REEL BASEBALL

BASEBALL'S GOLDEN ERA THE WAY AMERICA WITNESSED IT—

In the Movie Newsreels

LES KRANTZ

with DVD Hosted by

JOE GARAGIOLA

Doubleday

New York   London   Toronto   Sydney   Auckland

Contributing Writers:
Bill Chastain, Marty Strasen, Rob Rains

All the photographs were provided by AP Wide World Photos
except the following: page 72 and page 88, which are from
the National Baseball Hall of Fame, Library, Cooperstown, NY.

Book design and cover concept by Les Krantz
Art direction by Gene Dahlberg
Page composition by Diana Watkins

Cataloging-in-Publication Data
is on file with the Library of Congress.

ISBN-13: 978-0-385-51886-4
ISBN-10: 0-385-51886-2

PRINTED IN SINGAPORE

1 3 5 7 9 10 8 6 4 2

First Edition

———— ⟋⟍⟋⟍⟋⟍⟋⟍⟋⟍ ————

To Stan "the Man" Musial, Joltin' Joe,

and all the "Boys of Summer"

whom I worshipped as a youth

———— ⟋⟍⟋⟍⟋⟍⟋⟍ ————

ACKNOWLEDGMENTS

The author is particularly grateful to his contributing writers, who are listed on the copyright page; Charlie Conrad, Executive Editor at Doubleday; his assistant, Alison Presley; Jack Piantino; Tim Knight; and Joe Garagiola.

———— ⟋⟍⟋⟍⟋⟍⟋⟍ ————

CONTENTS

Pittsburgh's Bill Mazeroski wins the 1960 fall classic with a home run in the bottom of the ninth of Game 7 — the only seventh-game walk-off homer in World Series history.

CONTENTS

Midget Eddie Gaedel pinch-hits for the St. Louis Browns, July 19, 1951.

FOR LOVE OF THE GAME

THE BABE

The Yankees retire No. 3, as the "Sultan of Swat" reviews the grandstands one last time in uniform.

STAR POWER

CONTENTS

The already famous Satchel Paige, former legend of the Negro Leagues, gets his due, moving up to the big leagues, May 6, 1948.

LEGENDARY MOMENTS

"The Catch" — Willie Mays makes an amazing over-the-shoulder grab at the Polo Grounds in New York in Game 1 of the 1954 World Series.

CONTENTS

⌖⌖⌖⌖⌖⌖⌖⌖

GI Joe, DiMaggio that is, and Pee Wee Reese in their military baseball uniforms.

WARTIME BALL

WHEN THE RECORDS FELL

Out-swatting the Sultan, Roger Maris breaks the 34-year-old record established by Babe Ruth with his 61st homer, bagged on the last day of the season.

FOREWORD

BY YOGI BERRA

For me, this book *Reel Baseball* by Les Krantz is like déjà vu all over again.

Some of the newsreels on the DVD are the same ones we watched at the Columbia Theater when I was a kid on "The Hill," a mainly Italian section in St. Louis. We had this club called the Stags AC. We would walk up the neighborhood avenues, Macklind, over Botanical, and up Edwards, and we were at the Columbia show. It was a great trip for us. Joey (I still call Joe Garagiola Joey) lived right across the street from me. I lived at 5447 Elizabeth, and he lived at 5446. We always met to start the trip because this was a big deal for us.

All the way up we would talk about what we were going to see. We would really get excited when we talked about the newsreels, because sometimes we would get to see our favorite team, the St. Louis Cardinals, and especially our favorite player, Joe Medwick. Joey Garagiola would do most of the talking and try to imitate broadcaster France Laux telling us about "Ducky Wucky" Medwick with the bulging biceps from Cartaret, New Jersey. We didn't even know what bulging biceps were, but if Ducky had them, they were okay.

I'm glad Joey is going be a part of this book, which really makes me think of "the good old days." I still remember the 1934 World Series when the Cardinals played the Detroit Tigers, and the Detroit fans threw all that garbage at Medwick on the field. We cheered like crazy for him when we saw the newsreel because he was our guy. Now, with this book and DVD, I can watch that as many times as I want. You know what's great? Joey will talk about what you will be seeing, and then we'll hear the guys who were on the newsreel when we saw them, like Mel Allen.

I was lucky to play for the Yankees. I joined them at the end of the season in 1946 and stayed through 1963. We played in the World Series 14 times—you can count them— and we won the Series 10 times. I played in 75 World Series

games, and I'm proud of that record because that's more than anybody else, and I was the catcher in most of those games. That leads me to one of the great thrills for me, and a great newsreel. It was Don Larsen's perfect game in the 1956 World Series.

Even when I see just a newspaper picture, I start to remember everything about that game. Now to see it on a newsreel, I'll remember everything for sure. It was 50 years ago, on October 8. Larsen had good control that day and it was an easy game to call. He didn't shake off one pitch all day. I put the fingers down and he threw that pitch. What was funny was that nobody wanted to jinx him, so nobody would talk to him on the bench. He told me later that he knew he had a special game going because nobody was talking to him.

The other funny thing was when he struck out Dale Mitchell to end the game, I ran out to the mound and jumped into his arms. Usually, it's the pitcher who jumps into the catcher's arms, but I'm glad I beat him jumping because he was so big he would've buried me. On the DVD, check out the great jump I made.

There's a lot of things that happened that I'm going to enjoy, like watching Mickey and Roger hitting home runs and Lou Gehrig's speech. How about Willie Mays' great catch in the World Series, and Ted Williams hitting that eephus pitch in the All-Star Game? I got to tell you, I'm going to enjoy a lot of great baseball, but I'm not sure about seeing Mazeroski's home run that beat us in 1960. I was the left fielder that day, and I saw the ball go flying over my head.

Then there was Sandy Amoros' catch on the ball I hit to left field in Game 7 of the 1955 World Series. It should have been at least a double instead of a double play. I'll tell you a couple things. First, how come he was playing me near the left-field line? I was a pull hitter. Number two, if he wasn't a left-handed thrower and had the glove on his right hand, I don't think he could've caught that ball. Check it out.

I can't complain, because I had a great time playing in the big leagues. When I play the DVD, I get to go back and think about the days growing up with the guys and going to the Columbia show and seeing the newsreels, except that this time I'm in some of them. *Reel Baseball* is a terrific way for me and Joe and every fan to relive these great memories. I know you're going to enjoy this book, and with Joey's narration you'll get an idea of what it's like when the two of us talk baseball.

Yogi Berra

Yogi Berra, New York Yankee, holds a ball pitched to him in his 2,000th Major League game at Yankee Stadium, June 9, 1962.

INTRODUCTION

BY LES KRANTZ

When I was in high school, my friend Sidney Wasserman asked me if I'd be interested in going on a job interview. Being a lazy kid, my inclination was to say no, but there was much more to his offer. Going along with us would be our crowd—Bernie Goodman, Jerry Shanfeld, Howard Bushman and Alan Boime. That made it more palatable, but the guys were just the proverbial icing on the cake.

The job interview was with a company called St. Louis Usher Service. The venue was the old Sportsman Park in St. Louis, which by the 1960s was renamed Busch Stadium, after Augie Busch, the Cardinals' owner. That's where they played ball. The interview was for a job as an usher at the Park, a dream job that anyone would kill to get.

Well, I got it!

My workstation as an usher was right behind home plate. Not only did many of the players' families sit there, but the elevator to the broadcast booth was right behind my back. Legendary sportscaster Harry Caray said hello to me all the time.

I was no ordinary usher. I maintained a cache of baseballs that I'd scoop up from the bleachers during batting practice. Some of my colleagues had them too. They'd sell them to fans, sometimes faking autographs. But I was honest, no phony autographs, yet I made a tidy profit from them. I made it a point to know who hit the balls into bleachers and I would sell them, making the reliance that the ball was hit by various players. Stan Musial's were the most treasured. I also had some that were belted out by Bill Mazeroski, Hank Aaron, Duke Snider, Willie Mays, Roberto Clemente, Ted Kluszewksi, the greats! They'd fetch a buck a ball and as a supplement to the $4.75 I was paid per game, I was living a dream, getting paid to do what I'd almost certainly do for free.

One day in 1962 I had the distinct privilege of not only seeing, but actually talking to Casey Stengel. It was the season opener in a historic year in baseball, the beginning of the expansion teams, when the American and National Leagues went from eight teams to 10 in each league. Casey was looking like he was in shock. The Cardinals had beat his brand new Mets team by a wide margin . . . in their very first game.

"Hey Case," I said, leaning over to him at the locker room entrance. "They ain't exactly the Yanks, are they?"

"Nope," he replied. "They ain't." End of conversation.

I was so elated that he'd even acknowledged me, you'd have thought that I had just had a heart to heart with the President of the United States.

Seeing Casey Stengel was a huge deal for me. Before that night, I had never even set eyes on an American Leaguer, though Casey was obviously now managing the brand new National League team. Of course, I knew of the legends of the American League, but after the Browns left St. Louis to become the Baltimore Orioles, I was only able to see National League teams play in St. Louis; Even worse, most Americans of that era never even saw a major-league game, not live.

For most of the "Golden Era of Baseball," major-league baseball was played in only 12 U.S. cities, 11 of them east of the Mississippi River, and all of them north of the Mason-Dixon Line. Because of the big league's geographic quirks, over 80% of America watched major-league baseball only on the silver screen—in the movie newsreels. Made by Fox Movie Tone, Universal, and other studios that specialized in filming news events, the newsreels were "shorts," five to ten minutes of world news that was shown preceding the feature film.

With no television during most of the game's Golden Era, even East Coast fans with big league teams witnessed most baseball action of the day in "the reels" at movie theaters. It was here in cinema that the nation fell in love with "the Babe," "Joltin' Joe," "Stan the Man," and all the baseball greats. It was in movie newsreels that even the most ardent baseball fans saw them for the very first time. And it would be the only place that millions of fans would ever see them in action, versus captured in still photographs. In sum, the popularity of baseball and the movie newsreels were inextricably linked. It was because of this symbiotic relationship that baseball achieved its status as the national pastime, elevating the "boys of summer" to their legendary status in popular culture.

Reel Baseball looks at "the national pastime" through the prism of movie newsreels, much like America did during the Golden Era of Baseball. The content is derived from celluloid; that is, the text is a narrative about the most popular subjects of baseball newsreels that exemplify how they catapulted the game to its high priesthood in American pop culture during its Golden Era. It is an enchanting and magical trip through time that begins in 1933, when the first All-Star Game was played and concludes in 1965, with the opening of the Houston Astrodome, when modern stadiums and AstroTurf became the new trend. It was also in 1965 that newsreels ceased production, ending both the movie newsreel era and the Golden Era of Baseball.

But they still live, in my heart, and now in this book. I hope you'll enjoy the memories as much as Joe, Yogi, and I did.

Les Krantz

Sportsman Park was home to both the St. Louis Cardinals and the St. Louis Browns in 1944 when this photo was taken at the World Series, in which the two St. Louis teams battled for the Championship. It was here that *Reel Baseball* author Les Krantz got his first job decades later when it had been renamed Busch Stadium.

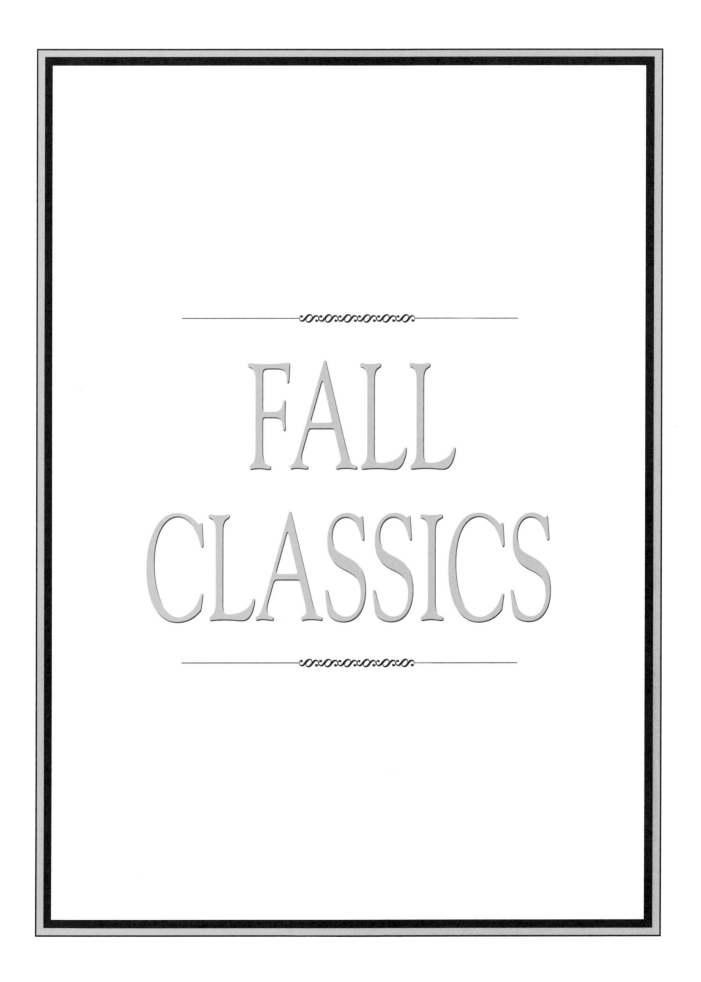

FALL CLASSICS

CHAPTER 1

LUCKY DUCKY

1934 WORLD SERIES

October 3-9, 1934 – Detroit: Before the St. Louis Cardinals and Detroit Tigers met in the World Series, star pitchers Dizzy Dean and his brother Paul Dean were invited to have breakfast with automobile pioneer Henry Ford in nearby Dearborn, Michigan. The Ford Motor Company had agreed to spend $100,000 to sponsor the radio broadcasts of the Series games to a nationwide audience.

pussycats out of your Tigers."

Dean and his 20-year-old brother, Paul, did just that by combining their pitching skills for all four St. Louis wins, as the Cardinals stopped the Tigers in seven games to win the World Series.

Never one to back away from a challenge or question his own ability, Dean won the first and seventh games, while his brother won games three and

A group of baseball's biggest names pose in Detroit on October 3, 1934, before the opening game of the Cardinals/Tigers World Series. Dizzy Dean, ace pitcher for the Cards, is on the left, with player/manager Frankie Frisch next to him. Babe Ruth is in the middle. Detroit's Mickey Cochrane, also a playing manager, is next to Ruth, and Schoolboy Rowe, the Tigers' star pitcher, is at right.

Despite being told what to say and how he should act, Dizzy Dean ignored those warnings and greeted Ford by saying, "Put 'er there, Henry. I'm sure glad to be here 'cause I heard so much about you, but I'm sorry I'm a-gonna have to make

six. Dizzy Dean earned an 8-3 win in the opening game. After the Tigers won Game 2 in the 12th inning, the Series moved to St. Louis, where Paul Dean picked up a 4-1 win. After a Detroit win evened the Series at two games each, the Tigers proved that

Dizzy Dean was human after all, by earning a 3-1 victory that put them one win away from winning the Series back in their hometown.

The Dean brothers were waiting, however, as Paul Dean threw a complete game, scattering seven hits, as the Cardinals won 4-3 to force the decisive seventh game. That was when Dizzy Dean took over. Dean's seventh game win came on only one day of rest; he shut out the Tigers on six hits as the Cardinals pounded the Tigers 11-0, ruining Detroit's attempts to win in its first Series appearance since 1909.

"I've got to keep up with Paul," Dean said before the game. "I'd like to win anyhow, I always like to win, but I can't let Paul down. He carried us to the seventh game. It's my time now, and if I have to I'll just throw my arm off to show the two Deans still move together. I wouldn't let Paul down for the world."

Luckily, Dean had a little margin for error in the deciding seventh game, as the Cardinals' offense — including Dean — erupted for seven third-inning runs to blow the game open. Dean had two hits himself in the inning.

Theater in New York.

Dean and his teammates — except for outfielder Joe Medwick — celebrated wildly after the victory. Medwick, the center of controversy during the game, was confined to his hotel room with seven bodyguards from the Detroit police department.

With the Cardinals ahead 7-0 going into the sixth, Medwick slammed a triple and slid hard into Tigers third baseman Marv Owen. Some observers thought Owen attempted to spike Medwick, who then raised his spikes in retaliation. The two scuffled briefly, but umpire Bill Klem soon restored order and the inning ended without further incident.

When Medwick attempted to take his defensive position in left field for the bottom of the sixth, however, he was greeted by anything and everything the 20,000 angry Detroit fans packed into the outfield bleachers at Navin Field could find to throw at him. The assault included pop bottles, oranges, apples, other fruit and rolled-up newspapers.

Workers cleared the debris after Medwick retreated toward the infield, but each time he

Gathered in the clubhouse after their 4-3 triumph over the Detroit Tigers, four key men in the Cardinals' machine celebrate their victory in the sixth game of the World Series, October 8, 1934. From left to right, Dizzy Dean; his brother Paul, who won his own game with a single; manager Frank Frisch; and catcher Bill DeLancey.

Dean's performance in the World Series, following his 30 victories in the regular season and combined with his personal charm, made him an early marketing phenomenon. He would go on to earn more than $40,000 in endorsements, personal appearances and banquet speeches in the winter following the 1934 season. Consumers would soon be able to buy a Dizzy Dean candy bar, Dizzy Dean overalls, a Dizzy Dean shirt and a Dizzy Dean watch. Dean and his brother received a $5,000 fee, more than Babe Ruth had received, for a one-week vaudeville stint at the Roxy

attempted to retake his position, the assault was renewed. Finally, Commissioner Kennesaw M. Landis summoned Medwick, Owen and the two managers, Frankie Frisch and Mickey Cochrane, to his box seat. Landis asked Owen if he had done anything to provoke Medwick's hard slide and when he said no, Landis ordered Medwick out of the game. That gave the Detroit fans something to cheer about, but not for long, as Dean and his teammates quickly closed out the victory.

The 1934 season marked the final year for Babe

Ruth in Yankee pinstripes, but the performance of Dean — who reached 30 wins by earning four victories in the final nine days of the season as he led the Cardinals to the pennant — gave the nation's baseball fans a new idol. Dean's status even reached legendary level when he was inserted into the fourth game of the Series as a pinch runner for catcher Spud Davis. On a ground ball, Dean went into second base standing up, and the relay throw from shortstop Billy Rogell hit Dean in the head.

Dean was carried off the field on a stretcher and taken to a St. Louis hospital for X-rays. Questioned after the game about his brother's condition, Paul

St. Louis' Pepper Martin pulls into third base during the 1934 All-Star Game in New York City. During that fall's World Series against Detroit, Martin batted .355 and scored eight runs in the seven games.

Dean said, "All he was doing was talking, just talking." Asked what he said, Paul said, "He wasn't saying anything, he was just talking."

The headline in the next day's newspaper had a double meaning: "X-Rays of Dean's Head Show Nothing."

Dean wasn't the country's only celebrity, however. Moviegoers that year were enthralled with the performance of Clark Gable in *It Happened One Night* and rejoiced at the animated character Donald Duck, who made his film debut just as the nation was trying to crawl out of the throes of the Depression.

HOW DEAN BECAME DIZZY

Dizzy Dean poses with movie siren Clara Bow at Sportman's Park in St. Louis in 1937.

Jay Hanna Dean was born on January 16, 1910, in Lucas, Arkansas, but he might never have achieved his national notoriety if he had not been given his famous nickname.

Dean enlisted in the Army when he was 16 years old, lying about his age by two years, but quickly found out it was a lot more work than he expected. It wasn't until he was assigned to kitchen duty, and began playing baseball for the unit team, that he became comfortable.

Legend has it that in August 1927, Sgt. James Brought, who was also the manager for Dean's team, was marching two platoons past the barracks when he saw Dean flinging freshly peeled potatoes at garbage can lids. Brought reportedly ran over to Dean and yelled, "You dizzy SOB."

The nickname spread, and it stuck. Over the next several months, Dean became known more as Dizzy Dean than Jay Dean. On April 17, 1928, after Dean had pitched for the unit team and struck out 17 batters from St. Mary's University, San Antonio newspapers first referred to him as "Dizzy Dean, the star twirler" for the Army team.

In his biography of Dean published in 1992, *Diz* author Robert Gregory quoted Brought as saying, "He was the laziest and most irresponsible soldier in the history of the U.S. Army and the biggest liar from here to the Rio Grande. There were times I know if that .45 I was wearing had ammo I would've shot the SOB full of holes, even if he was the greatest pitcher I ever saw."

Two weeks after Dean left the Army in 1929, he was pitching for the best local semipro team in the San Antonio area, where he was quickly discovered by a part-time scout for the Cardinals, Don Curtis. Curtis signed him to a contract with the Cardinals' Houston, Texas farm team for $300 a month. Dean joined the team in March, 1930, and soon was on his way to the major leagues.

CHAPTER 2

THE YANKEE MACHINE

1939 WORLD SERIES

October 4-8, 1939 — Cincinnati: The New York Yankees reported to spring training in St. Petersburg in 1939 with three consecutive World Series titles under their belt. No team in major-league history had ever managed to run that string to four consecutive titles, which was the goal of the most famous franchise in sports history entering the season.

home runs, 152 RBI and a .354 batting average. Meanwhile, DiMaggio joined the Yankees in 1936 and complemented Gehrig nicely with a .323 batting average, 29 home runs and 125 RBI. The California-born rookie helped lead the team to victory in the Subway Series showdown with the New York Giants later that year. Showing the flexibility to pound their opponent — 18-4 and

Yankees outfielder Charley "King Kong" Keller has just crashed into Cincinnati Reds catcher Ernie Lombardi, scoring in the 10th inning of the clinching Game 4 of the 1939 World Series. Lombardi was so stunned by the collision that he failed to recover in time to stop the batter, Joe DiMaggio, who had singled, from scoring as well.

Integral to the Yankees winning three straight World Series titles was a lineup consisting of Frank Crosetti, Bill Dickey, Joe DiMaggio, Lou Gehrig, and Tony Lazzeri. Perhaps of greater significance was the fact that the lineup did not include Babe Ruth. Lefty Gomez and Red Ruffing led the equally impressive Yankees pitching staff.

Their incredible run began in 1936. Gehrig remained the cornerstone of the lineup with 49

13-5 wins in Games 2 and 6 — and win the close ones — 2-1 win in Game 3 — the Yankees dispatched the Giants in six games.

In 1937, the two New York teams once again faced each other in the World Series — and the result was just the same. This time, however, it took just five games for the Yankees to fend off the Giants' challenge for the World Series title.

In 1938 the Chicago Cubs took on the

Yankees, who easily outclassed the Cubs in four games to retain their World Series title. Looking for their fourth consecutive championship in 1939, the Yankees had obstacles to overcome when they reported to spring training. First, they had heavy hearts from the death of team owner Jake Ruppert, who died of phlebitis in January of 1939. Even more troubling was the precarious status of Lou Gehrig.

Gehrig, known to all as baseball's "Iron Horse" for playing in more than 2,000 consecutive games, complained of fatigue for the length of spring training. On May 2, 1939, Gehrig's streak of playing 2,130 straight games came to a sad end, when he withdrew from the starting lineup; he could no longer field or hit with any power. Everyone's suspicions that the great first baseman

the Chicago White Sox in the Series that came to be known as the notorious "Black Sox Scandal," after the White Sox sold out to gamblers.

The tandem of Bucky Walters and Paul Derringer, who had 27 and 25 wins between them, bolstered the Reds' pitching. As for the Yankees, Gehrig was with the team in uniform, but only as the team's captain and not as a player available for duty.

Derringer pitched Game 1 and was opposed by Ruffing, who had just completed his fourth consecutive 20-win season. And the veteran Yankee right-hander responded with a four-hit, 2-1 victory. The game had been tied at 1-1 in the bottom of the ninth when Charlie Keller tripled to right center field. Although Derringer intentionally walked DiMaggio, Dickey cinched Game 1 for the

New York manager Joe McCarthy (bottom right) enjoys his players' glee following the Yankees' fourth straight World Series win, October 8, 1939. Coach Art Fletcher (upper right) leads the team cheer as catcher Buddy Rosar raises his cap.

was sick were confirmed at the Mayo Clinic on June 21, when it was discovered he was suffering from amyotrophic lateral sclerosis, a fatal neuromuscular disease.

Babe Dahlgren took Gehrig's place at first base and responded by hitting .235, with 15 home runs and 89 RBI. Still, the Yankees managed to take the American League flag with a 106-45 record, good enough to finish 17 games in front of the second-place Red Sox. Their opponents in the fall classic were the Cincinnati Reds, who were in their first World Series since 1919, when they had defeated

Yankees with a winning single through the Reds' infield.

Walters started Game 2 and once again, a Yankees pitcher outdueled a Reds ace. This time Monte Pearson turned the trick. The Yankees right-hander held the Reds without a hit for seven innings — leaving Pearson six outs from becoming the first pitcher in World Series history to throw a no-hitter. Pearson retired the first hitter in the eighth before Ernie Lombardi singled to break up the no-hit bid. Pearson allowed just one more hit and finished with a two-hit, 4-0 complete game that saw Dahlgren boost the offense with a double and home run.

The Series shifted to Cincinnati's Crosley Field for Game 3 and the Reds broke out their bats with 10 hits, which doubled the Yankees' total of five. Unfortunately for the Reds, the Yankees had significant hitting on their side. Keller had two home runs, while DiMaggio and Dickey had one each to lead a 7-3 Yankees win and put the defending champions in a commanding position entering Game 4.

Game 4 stood scoreless at the start of the seventh inning. Then, Keller and Dickey hit home runs off Derringer, who was making his second start of the Series. Steve Sundra began his third inning of work for the Yankees in the bottom half of the seventh, but the Reds would not die easy as they

The Reds failed to score in the ninth, sending the game to extra innings. With runners on first and third and one out, DiMaggio again had a chance to shine when he batted in the 10th. And "Joltin' Joe" came through with a single to right field that right fielder Ival Goodman botched, which allowed the runner from first to score. Lombardi could not handle Goodman's throw to the plate and Keller knocked him down, allowing the ball to get away. Before the ball could be retrieved, DiMaggio scored easily while the Reds' catcher lay where he'd gone down on a play that came to be known as "Schnozz's snooze."

Deflated, the Reds had the tying run at bat three times in the bottom of the 10th, but failed to do anything against Murphy, who held on to protect the Yankees' 7-4 lead and preserve the

Red Ruffing, Yankees right-hander, and Paul Derringer, mainstay of the Cincinnati Reds, pitched complete games in Game 1 of the 1939 World Series. New York beat Derringer 2-1 on a ninth-inning single by Bill Dickey.

touched Sundra for three unearned runs. The Reds then added a run in the eighth off Johnny Murphy to take a 4-2 lead into the ninth, when they had a chance to win — until shortstop Billy Myers made an error on what appeared to be a double-play ball. The Yankees scored on the play and then tied the game when DiMaggio beat the throw on a bang-bang play at the plate.

sweep.

The Yankees had accomplished the unimaginable by taking their fourth consecutive world championship. In doing so the Yankees won 13 of their last 14 World Series games, establishing that Yankees team as one of the best in baseball history.

CHAPTER 3

BACK IN THE DRIVER'S SEAT

1945 WORLD SERIES

Top: Tigers hurler Hal Newhouser receives a gold watch from *The Sporting News* on August 12, 1945. The award honored his selection as *TSN*'s 1944 "Pitcher of the Year." Newhouser went 29-9 in 1944, then followed up with a 25-9 mark the next season. Bottom: Chicago's star hurler Claude Passeau threw a one-hit shutout in Game 3 of the 1945 World Series, winning 3-0. Only Tigers first baseman Rudy York's second-inning single and a base on balls to Bob Swift kept Passeau from perfection. During a 13-year major-league career, Passeau won 162 games.

October 3-10, 1945 — Chicago: When the World Series matchup between the Chicago Cubs and the Detroit Tigers was set, Chicago sportswriter Warren Brown was asked for his prediction about the Series' outcome.

"I don't think either of them can win," Brown quipped.

The talent in the major leagues had been severely diluted because of World War II, and even though the war was now over, many players still were completing their military service. Stan Musial of the Cardinals missed all of the 1945 season — his absence was one of the reasons why the Cubs were able to overtake St. Louis and win the NL pennant.

The Tigers players, who were older than the players on many other teams, included slugging first baseman Hank Greenberg, who had rejoined the team post-VE Day, after serving four years in the Army; and pitcher Virgil Trucks, who was discharged from the Navy after the Japanese surrendered in August. Trucks returned in time to pitch the final game of the season, clinching the pennant.

Because of travel restrictions established during the war — the same restrictions that had canceled the 1945 All-Star Game — the first three games of the Series were scheduled to be played in Detroit. Whatever remaining games were necessary would be played at Chicago's Wrigley Field.

That arrangement seemed to favor the Tigers, but those thoughts quickly disappeared when the Cubs roughed up ace Hal Newhouser in Game 1, rolling to a 9-0 victory.

A three-run homer by Greenberg carried the Tigers to a 4-1 victory in the second game, but Chicago regained the edge the next day, when pitcher Claude Passeau threw a one-hitter in a Cubs' 3-0 triumph. Only two Detroit batters reached base: Rudy York on a second-inning single, and Bob Swift on a sixth-inning walk.

Opposite: Detroit's Hank Greenberg (crossing the plate) has just homered in Game 2 of the 1945 World Series against the Cubs. Greenberg's three-run shot helped the Tigers win 4-1. Greenberg spent half the season in the service, but he did bat .311 with 13 home runs in 78 games to help Detroit win the AL title.

Infielder Eddie Mayo of Detroit scores the Tigers' final run in their 9-3 win over the Cubs in Game 7 of the 1945 World Series. Mayo scored on Hank Greenberg's sacrifice fly; Greenberg knocked in seven runs in the series.

As the Series shifted to Chicago, the Cubs were only two victories away from winning the World Series for the first time since 1908. Those two wins, however, proved elusive.

Before the fourth game, starlet June Haver visited both benches and planted a kiss on Cubs manager Charlie Grimm's cheek. Scalpers were getting as much as $200 for box seats, and grandstand seats were going for $75 a pair. Four men were even arrested before the fifth game for trying to sell bleacher tickets for $5 and $6 each.

Unfortunately, the Cubs did not give their fans much to cheer about in losing both the fourth and fifth games. Detroit rode the pitching of Dizzy Trout to a 4-1 win in Game 4, and Newhouser bounced back with an 8-4 win in the fifth game.

Needing a win in Game 6 to stay alive in the Series, the Cubs built a 7-3 lead in the eighth. Passeau was throwing another gem but had to come out of the game when he injured a finger trying to knock down a line drive in the seventh.

Relievers Hank Wyse and Ray Prim couldn't hold the lead, and the Tigers rallied for four runs in the eighth, capped by Greenberg's homer. The game went into extra innings. Hank Borowy, who had started and pitched five innings for the Cubs the day before, came out of the bullpen to throw four shutout innings as the teams battled until the

THE GOAT OF THE SERIES

Did the Cubs lose the 1945 World Series because of a curse?

When the Series shifted to Chicago for the fourth game of the Series, a man named William Sianis, who owned a popular tavern, had two box seat tickets for the game and brought his pet goat with him as his date. The ushers tried to keep Sianis and the goat out of the ballpark, but he made it inside and actually paraded the goat around on the field. Sianis pinned a note on the goat that read, "We've Got Detroit's Goat."

During the game, Cubs owner Phil Wrigley found out what was going on, apparently when the smell from the goat made it up to the owner's box, and had Sianis and the goat ejected from the stadium. Before he left the stadium, Sianis reportedly put a curse on the Cubs, which said the team would never win another pennant or play in another World Series.

After the Tigers won the deciding seventh game of the Series, Sianis reportedly sent a telegram to Wrigley that read, "Who smells now?"

12th inning. Stan Hack's RBI double finally gave the Cubs the win, forcing the deciding seventh game. It was the first seventh game in the history of the Cubs franchise.

The excitement in Chicago was at a fever pitch. The 36,000-plus reserved seats sold out in 3 hours, making it only the second pregame sellout of a seventh game in history.

Excitement was not just limited to Chicago. The Armed Forces Radio Network broadcast the World Series around the world. Many soldiers reportedly rose at 3 a.m. in the Philippines to listen to the broadcasts. For the first time since 1941,

spent, and after the first three Detroit batters all reached on singles, Grimm pulled Borowy and brought in Paul Derringer; however, Derringer proved to be almost as ineffective as the exhausted Borowy. The Tigers scored five runs in the first inning, deflating the hopes of the crowd of 41,590 almost before they had a chance to get settled in their seats.

The final score was 9-3. Newhouser, pitching on two days' rest, scattered 10 hits in cruising to the victory and extending the Cubs' World Series' losing streak for another year.

"We were beaten by a good club, but not a

Phil Cavaretta, manager Charlie Grimm, and Bill Nicholson of the Cubs (left to right) flank a group of servicemen, blinded in combat, prior to the opening game of the 1945 World Series.

players shared in the $100,000 fee paid by the Gillette Safety Razor Blade Co. to sponsor the radio broadcasts. For the previous three years, that money had been added to baseball's contribution to the war charities and funds.

The win in Game 6 proved costly for the Cubs, however, as Borowy had been Charlie Grimm's expected starter in the seventh game. The teams had a day of rest between the sixth and seventh games, and Grimm decided to go with Borowy anyway as his starter.

It was immediately obvious that Borowy was

better club than I have," Grimm said. "Just pitching beat us, but these guys are still champs in my book. They gave it everything they had.

"Borowy didn't have a lot when he warmed up and I knew it, but I wanted to give it a try. I thought maybe he'd get by until he warmed up to the job."

That didn't happen, however, and Cubs fans were forced to spend yet another winter lamenting how close they had come to victory. Little did they know that their wait for a World Series title was only just beginning.

CHAPTER 4

SLAUGHTER'S MAD DASH

1946 WORLD SERIES, GAME 7

October 15, 1946 — St. Louis: This Mississippi River town is no stranger to the World Series. In 1945, after the exuberance of the Japanese surrender, the celebratory mood of St. Louisians went straight downriver. Though the war was won, the Cardinals weren't in the 1945 Series — the first time the "Redbirds" hadn't made it there since the Japanese bombed Pearl Harbor.

But now, a year later at Sportsman's Park, one of the grand old ballparks of the era, the stadium was abuzz. The Boston Red Sox were taking the field in Game 7 — the best numbered game of all if you like suspense, and the air was thick with it now. To make it even better, this was the year that baseball returned to normal, with hundreds of players back from their wartime service. Among the returnees was former Navy pilot Ted Williams, the 1946 American League MVP, who suited up in Game 7.

Top: Babe Ruth, now retired and here to see the game, had been to a few World Series himself. Bottom: St. Louis Cardinal Joe Garagiola broke his finger in the 6th inning and could not finish the final game of the series. Right: Slaughter slides into home after his lightning-quick dash from first base, scoring the Series-winning run.

Opposite: St. Louis Cardinals' Hall of Famers (from right to left) Stan Musial, Joe "Ducky" Medwick, and Enos Slaughter. Though Medwick played for the Dodgers in 1946, he was on and off the Cardinal roster during the 1940s, due to being traded to several ball clubs. He returned to the Cardinals in 1947.

Stan Musial, who also served in the Navy during the war, took the field for St. Louis. Before his military service, Musial had won the 1943 National League batting title, cracking .357. Naysayers maintained that the rail-thin Polish boy from Pennsylvania won the crown only because the real hitting and hurling talents were in the military. But the Cardinals slugger won the 1946 NL batting crown with an even better .365 average — and that was with all the greats back on the field. He showed his critics! In 1941, Musial's teammate Enos Slaughter had led the league in hits. He was here too for Game 7. So was the Cards rookie catcher, 21-year-old Joe Garagiola, not to mention Babe Ruth, who was in the stands to watch the game.

There was a goat here today too. Well, he wasn't a goat yet, but he would be by the eighth inning. His name was Johnny Pesky, and for 60 years Red Sox fans would hold a bitter gripe against him. It went like this: "Pesky held the [adjective deleted] ball!"

The accusation was in reference to a decisive play that would take place in this championship game when Sox shortstop Pesky — as some judged — hadn't relayed the ball quickly enough from center field to home plate, thereby allowing Enos Slaughter to score the game-winning run. In St. Louis, though, they don't talk about Pesky much. Instead, Cardinals fans pay homage to Slaughter for making his "mad dash" from first base all the way to home plate on a single that skeptics say was really a double. Harry "The Hat" Walker was the hitter who drove in Slaughter. Over a decade later, Pesky would serve him as a coach with Pittsburgh.

Boston scored first in Game 7 with one run in the top of the first, but St. Louis came back with one in the second and added two more in the fifth. Dramatically, the Red Sox tied the game in the top of the eighth when Dom DiMaggio doubled off the screen in right-center, driving in two pinch hitters who had preceded him. DiMaggio's hit had tied the game, but he injured himself trying to extend the double into a triple and had to leave the game. Dom knew he had no good reason to stay at second; Williams was up next, and the Cardinals simply would have walked the big guy. Replacing DiMaggio in center field was Leon Culberson. Had DiMaggio been in center, the outcome of the game might well have been different.

In the bottom of the eighth, Slaughter singled, but reliever Bob Klinger retired the next two batters. The first out came on a botched sacrifice bunt that Klinger caught in the air while running toward the first base line. The next batter flew out to left. With two out, Slaughter decided to make things happen on the basepaths. Enos bolted for second before Klinger released the pitch, and he

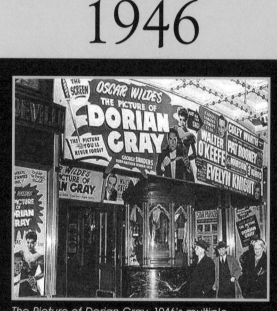

1946

The Picture of Dorian Gray, 1946's multiple Academy Award—winning feature, shared many movie screens with the World Series newsreels.

WHAT IT COST IN 1946
With the war over, both baseball and the rest of the world were beginning to return to normal. Cars, tires, gasoline, sugar, and even nylons (at 85 cents a pair) were readily available. Below is a sampling of what things cost in 1946:

- Movie Ticket: 35 cents in St. Louis, 40 cents in Boston, 50 cents in New York
- Yankee Stadium, General Admission: 90 cents
- Parking Near Stadium: 25 cents
- Hot Dog: 15 cents
- Hamburger: 20 cents
- Coca-Cola: 5 cents
- Bottle of Beer: 15 cents

NEWSREELS OF THE DAY: Newsreels screened highlights of the Nuremberg Trials, for which the last reel and verdict were completed about the same time (October) as the World Series. The year began with reporting on the newly formed United Nations and the worrisome Argentinean fascist government under Juan Peron. Movie audiences heard a newly coined term, "mushroom-shaped cloud," in newsreels reporting on the Bikini Atoll A-bomb test.

was a third of the way there by the time the ball reached the plate. Walker (a .237 hitter for the regular season) drilled the ball sharply to left-center. Slaughter rounded the bag and headed to third. The ball wasn't hit that deep, but it was ideally positioned. Culberson ran over to field it, angling a bit deeper in the process.

No one would have expected Slaughter to try to score, yet he was almost to third by the time the Sox center fielder got to the ball. The proper play

second, but then noticed Slaughter making a mad dash to the plate. Surprised, he geared up and threw home, and a perfect bullet might yet have had the runner. But Slaughter was really too close to the plate, and Johnny's throw went about eight feet up the line. Walker took second base.

Suddenly, the Cardinals were up 4-3. They successfully though precariously protected the lead in the ninth inning despite a threat from Boston, as both Rudy York and Bobby Doerr singled to open

Left: Harry "The Hat" Walker, the man who got the eighth-inning hit that drove in Enos Slaughter from first base. Right: Johnny Pesky, who fielded Walker's hit. Did he hold the ball too long, or did Walker get a double rather than a single? The controversy is still unresolved.

for Culberson was to throw to Pesky, the cutoff man, who had moved out to the edge of the infield grass to take the throw. Pesky would have been expected to look to second base and then run the ball back in to hold Walker to a single while Slaughter pulled up at third. There didn't seem to be anything unusual about the play — and with no particular urgency and without any hesitation, Culberson "lofted the ball" to Pesky.

Pesky took the throw, looked first toward

the inning. Harry Brecheen shut the Sox down, though, and earned his third victory of the Series to win the world title for St. Louis. To make the feat that much more spectacular, he had pitched in Game 6 — all nine innings — just two days earlier.

A few days later, when the Movietone newsreel of Slaughter's baserunning was shown before the feature at St. Louis's premier movie house, the Fox Theatre, audiences threw popcorn high into the air, as if it were confetti, as Slaughter slid into home.

CHAPTER 5

THE COOKIE CRUMBLES

1947 WORLD SERIES, GAME 4

October 6, 1947 — New York: A changing landscape greeted the 1947 World Series between the New York Yankees and Brooklyn Dodgers. World War II was over and America's war heroes had returned from combat to pursue the American dream.

The 1947 World Series reflected progress in the fact it was the first World Series to be televised. More importantly, it was also the first fall classic in which

aggressive style of play. For his rookie season, Robinson had a batting average of .297, with 29 stolen bases.

Robinson's addition helped the Dodgers put away the St. Louis Cardinals and claim the National League pennant by five games. Other standouts for the Dodgers included Dixie Walker, Carl Furillo and Pete Reiser, leading the offense. Starters Ralph

Despite the efforts of guards, fans swarm onto the field at Yankee Stadium, October 6, 1947, celebrating the Yankees' 5-2 victory over the Brooklyn Dodgers. The Game 7 win clinched the World Series for the Bombers, the organization's 11th championship.

one of the teams had a black player on the roster: the Dodgers' Jackie Robinson. That year, Robinson had become the first black player to break Major League Baseball's color barrier. And while he felt the sting of racism at many stops during the season, the rookie infielder became a huge attraction, due to his

Branca, who went 21-12, and Joe Hatten, who won 17, led the pitching. Among the unheralded members of the Dodgers was 34-year-old former All-Star Cookie Lavagetto, whose 10-year career was drawing to a close; he batted just 69 times during the regular season and collected 18 hits.

In Brooklyn the Dodgers were lovingly known as "Dem Bums." In the World Series they represented the classic underdogs against the Yankees led by the great Joe DiMaggio, the Yankees' regal superstar.

The Yankees had nailed down the American League pennant with a 19-game winning streak that began in June and led to their winning the pennant by 12 games.

Unlike other Yankees teams that had inspired such nicknames as "Bronx Bombers" and "Murderer's Row," these Yankees lacked offense. DiMaggio was the only member of the team to reach 20 home runs. Superb pitching countered the team's lack of offense. Allie Reynolds led the way with 19 wins in his first season as a Yankee; Reynolds had previously played for the Indians. The rest of the staff included Spud Chandler, who led the league with a 2.46 ERA, and rookie Spec Shea. Shea had 14 wins, as did Joe Page, working in relief.

Given the untypical nature of this Yankees team, the Dodgers appeared to have a chance against their crosstown rival in the fall classic.

But Shea picked up the win in a 5-3 Yankees win in Game 1. Reynolds then kept the strong pitching going in a 10-3 win in Game 2 that saw the Yankee cobble together 15 hits. The Series moved to Ebbets Field for Game 3 and the Dodgers fought back to take a 9-8 victory, due largely to the Dodgers' six-run, second inning, paced by two-run doubles from Eddie Stanky and Furillo.

Yankees manager Bucky Harris looked over his available pitchers for Game 4 and chose Bill Bevens. It was a choice that many saw as odd, for Bevens had won just seven times in 20 decisions in 1947. But the decision clicked — in a roundabout way.

Bevens was effectively wild and would issue a World Series-record 10 walks — which led to the Dodgers scoring a run in the fifth inning after Bevins walked two and Pee Wee Reese grounded out to drive home a runner. Despite the sloppy nature of Bevens'

performance, he looked sharp retiring the side in order in the eighth. He took the mound in the ninth protecting a 2-1 lead — and the first no-hitter in World Series history.

Bevens could have had a bigger lead heading into the bottom of the ninth, but Tommy Henrich had grounded into an inning-ending doubleplay with the bases loaded to end the threat, without increasing the Yankees' lead.

Would Bevens complete his flawed masterpiece? If he did so, the Dodgers would go down 3-1 in the Series. The buzz inside Ebbets Field echoed an optimism that the home team could somehow find a way to pull out a win. The buzz subsided somewhat when Bruce Edwards flew out to lead off the ninth. Furillo then walked before Spider Jorgensen fouled out for the second out, putting Bevens on the doorstep of baseball immortality. One more out and Bevens' name would live forever in World Series history.

Dodgers manager Burt Shotton inserted Al Gionfriddo as a pinch runner for Furillo and Reiser as a pinch hitter for reliever Hugh Casey. Gionfriddo took off for second base, stumbling out of the gate when he started his journey. Fortunately for Gionfriddo, he had the element of surprise on his side. Yankees catcher Yogi Berra seemed the most surprised of all, raising to throw and pumping once before throwing late to second.

"I slipped on the very first step," Gionfriddo said afterward. "I thought I was a dead duck. To make up for it, when I came into second I didn't slide feet first. I just made a head-first dive for the bag. Somehow I made it. But I still think any kind of throw would have had me."

With first base open and Reiser at the plate with a 3-1 count, the Yankees intentionally walked Reiser. By willingly putting the potential winning run on base, the Yankees effectively broke one of the cardinal rules of baseball. The wheels of Shotton's mind

Al Gionfriddo, Brooklyn Dodgers substitute left fielder, turns his back to the plate and starts for the 415-foot marker, chasing Joe DiMaggio's long drive in the sixth inning of World Series Game 6 at Yankee Stadium on October 5, 1947. The ball was about to drop over the outfield fence for a three-run homer when Gionfriddo leaped and speared the ball spectacularly to end the inning. Oddly, this was Gionfriddo's last game in the major leagues.

continued to whirl. He inserted Eddie Miksis to run for Reiser, and then called upon Lavagetto to pinch-hit for Stanky.

Lavagetto watched Bevens' first pitch go by for ball one. Lavagetto swung at the next pitch, driving the outside fastball toward right field. Henrich ran after the ball, but couldn't get to it before it hit off the wall in the corner. Running on contact, Gionfriddo and Miksis scored easily, setting off a celebration inside Ebbets Field.

Dodgers players accorded Lavagetto a hero's treatment by carrying him off the field on their shoulders. Bevens' no-hitter — and victory — had

Cookie Lavagetto of the Dodgers laughs in the clubhouse at Brooklyn's Ebbets Field after breaking up Game 4 of the 1947 World Series on October 3. Lavagetto ended Yankees hurler Bill Bevens' bid for a no-hitter with a two-run, ninth-inning pinch double that won the game for the Dodgers, 3-2. The timely clout was Lavagetto's final major-league hit.

ended on one pitch. The Dodgers had tied the World Series at two games apiece.

While Brooklyn celebrated the unlikely victory by their neighborhood team in Game 4, the Yankees shook off the loss to take the Series in seven games, their first victory since 1943. After the World Series, neither Bevens nor Lavagetto ever played in another major-league game.

BEVENS' NEAR MISS

New York Yankee Pitcher Bill Bevens fires in the fourth inning of Game Four.

Floyd Clifford "Bill" Bevens was the unlikely choice of Yankee manager Bucky Harris to start Game 4 of the 1947 World Series against the Brooklyn Dodgers.

Standing six feet, three inches and weighing 210 pounds, the Hubbard, Oregon native had a 40-36 record with a 3.08 ERA in four major-league seasons for the Yankees when he got his fateful call against the Dodgers. In 1947, Bevens posted a 7-13 record with a 3.82 ERA — including 77 walks in 165 innings, which might have been a bellwether for his future.

Bevens was one out from history when Cookie Lavagetto spoiled the no-hit bid with a two-run double off the outfield wall to win the game. After the winning run scored, Bevens, who had been backing up the play at home, watched home plate umpire Larry Goetz brush off the plate.

"He was so wrapped up in the game he didn't even know it was over, but I sure did," Bevens would later say. Yankees catcher Yogi Berra called Bevens' near miss the best game he ever caught.

Bevens experienced arm problems the next season. He pitched some in the minor leagues before deciding to retire. His performance against the Dodgers was his last in the major leagues.

CHAPTER 6

BRAVE WARRIORS

1948 WORLD SERIES

October 11, 1948 — Boston: The American League had never seen a season quite like the one that transpired in 1948. When all the smoke cleared, the Cleveland Indians and the Boston Red Sox were locked in a tie for the pennant with identical 96-58 records.

Cleveland had experienced a whirlwind season of fun and excitement, much of which trickled down from the top, where maverick owner Bill Veeck created a colorful environment for baseball. Indians fans responded to the efforts of the home

American League's first black player, Larry Doby, as well as sluggers Ken Keltner and Joe Gordon.

Leading up to the great finish in 1949, the legendary Joe DiMaggio had carried the Yankees to a three-way tie with the Red Sox and Indians with only nine days remaining in the season. Ted Williams, arguably the greatest hitter in the history of the game, led the Red Sox. But it was the Indians who persevered in the American League's first-ever one-game playoff to decide the pennant in a game played at Boston's Fenway Park.

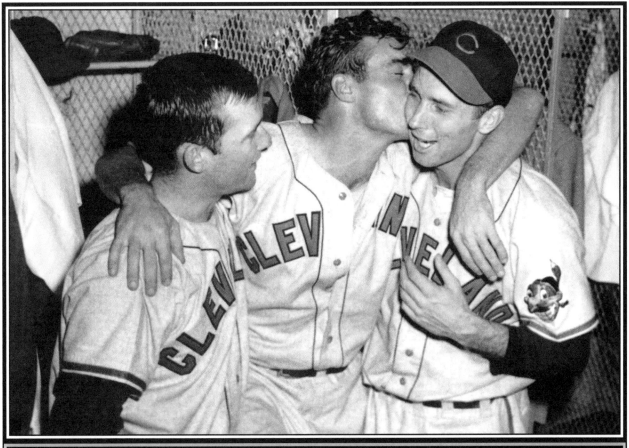

Cleveland Indians pitcher Gene Bearden embraces teammates Bob Lemon, left, and catcher Jim Hegan, right, after the sixth and final game of the World Series in Boston on Oct. 11, 1948. Lemon won the game and Bearden saved it. The Indians clinched the series with a 4-3 triumph over the Boston Braves.

team by pushing through the turnstiles in record fashion. Calling the shots on the field for the Indians was player-manager Lou Boudreau, who led the Indians with a .355 batting average while playing shortstop. He had a team that included the

Boudreau went 4-for-4, including two home runs to lead the offense, while 27-year-old rookie left-hander Gene Bearden, who had suffered head and knee injuries in World War II, picked up the win, his 20th of the season. With this victory, the

Cleveland Indians would make their second appearance in the World Series.

Because the Indians had finished their season in Boston, the Indians merely had to travel across town to meet their National League foe, the Boston Braves. The Braves had won the senior circuit's pennant by 6 1/2 games. Though they lacked the Indians' power, the Braves had five .300 hitters in a lineup that included Tommy Holmes, Mike McCormick and Jeff Heath.

Pitching drew the most attention heading into the 1948 fall classic and rightly so. Anchoring a

and held the Braves scoreless the final eight innings to lead a 4-1 Indians triumph and square the Series at one game each. Bearden followed with a five-hit shutout in Game 3 and chipped in a single and a double, scoring the Indians first run in a 2-0 win.

Steve Gromek started Game 4 for the Indians and once again the team received superlative pitching — their fourth consecutive complete game — along with a home run by Doby, en route to a 2-1 victory. The Indians were now one game shy of winning the World Series.

Lou Boudreau, at right, Cleveland Indians manager and shortstop, stands with manager Billy Southworth of the Boston Braves at Braves Field in Boston on October 6, 1948, prior to the opening game of the World Series. Boudreau was the AL's Most Valuable Player in 1948.

talented Indians staff was the trio of Bob Feller, Bob Lemon and Bearden. Boston was managed by Billy Southworth and had aces Warren Spahn and Johnny Sain, who had inspired the saying "Spahn and Sain and two days of rain."

In Game 1, Sain was pitted against Feller, who was making his World Series debut and receiving the sentimental accolades accorded a veteran of his stature. "Rapid Robert" was on his game, as was Sain. When the game moved into the bottom of the eighth, it remained scoreless. That's when Feller and Boudreau appeared to work a pickoff play at second base to perfection, only to have umpire Bill Stewart call pinch runner Phil Masi safe. Pictures capturing the play showed that Masi was out. Holmes then singled with two outs to give the Braves a 1-0 lead that held.

Lemon started the second game for the Indians

If a storybook ending were in the cards, it would have been having Feller finish off the Braves in Game 5 in front of a major-league record crowd of 86,288 at Cleveland Stadium. But sentimentality didn't interest the Braves in the least; they teed off on Feller in the fifth game, bouncing the right-hander with seven runs on eight hits in 6 1/3 innings. With one out in the fourth inning, Spahn came in to relieve Braves starter Nelson Potter and held the Indians scoreless the rest of the way in an 11-6 Braves' win.

The Braves' Bob Elliott hit two home runs in the game, making him only the second National League player to hit more than one home run during a Series game. The first with a pair of homers was Benny Kauff of the New York Giants during the 1917 World Series; there had already been 10 instances where an American League player hit two home runs.

Also of note, 42-year-old Satchel Paige became one of the five pitchers used by the Indians in Game 5. The Negro Leagues' legend signed a contract with the Indians in July of 1948 and compiled a 6-1 regular season record. The appearance by Paige, who retired both batters he faced, made him the first black pitcher to take the mound in a World Series.

The Braves' win showed that they still had a pulse, even though they trailed the Series three games to two.

The game remained tied until Gordon led off the sixth with a home run and the Indians added another run on a forced out. Eddie Robinson completed the Indians' scoring with a RBI single in the eighth to push the lead to 4-1.

Once again, the Braves' heart could not be discounted. They rallied for two runs on two doubles, a walk and a single in the eighth. But Bearden, who relieved Lemon with one out in the eighth, stabbed a grounder hit by McCormick to end the threat. Boston threatened again in the ninth, but the Indians got a much-needed double

Cleveland Indians pitcher Satchel Paige — a Negro Leagues veteran — who, as a 42-year-old rookie, helped his team win the American League pennant, became the first African-American to pitch in a World Series. He appeared during Game 5 of the 1948 World Series on October 5.

Boudreau sent Lemon to the mound to start Game 6 while the Braves came up with an empty chamber in their gun. Neither Spahn nor Sain nor rain was available for Game 6, so Bill Voiselle was sent to the mound.

Boudreau's RBI double in the third gave the Indians a 1-0 lead and Boston countered in the fourth on McCormick's RBI single to tie the game.

play before finally getting a fly ball to preserve the 4-3 Indians win.

Despite hitting just .199 as a team against the Braves, the Indians had benefited greatly from the contributions of Lemon, Bearden, Gromek, and Boudreau. In the end, they claimed their first World Series title since 1920.

CHAPTER 7

THE STAR-CROSSED SERIES

GIANT PREDICTIONS FOR DUROCHER

October 4-10, 1951 — New York: Oh, the story he could tell, manager Leo Durocher thought, if only his New York Giants could beat the Yankees in the 1951 World Series. Back in spring training in Florida, Durocher, pitcher Fred Fitzsimmons, and their wives had visited an astrologer who had made outrageous predictions — that were coming true.

"The astrologist, a nondescript middle-aged woman, told Fitz to change the number on his

of my life and end up winning everything."

Durocher and the gang had laughed at her predictions — until the Giants lost 11 straight games in April. At that point, Fitzsimmons decided to change his uniform number to five and start wearing purple underwear. By July 27, Durocher's birthday, the Giants were a half-game out of last place. Yet in epic fashion, Leo's boys won 39 of their last 47 games before winning a three-game playoff against Brooklyn

Left: Phil Rizzuto (left) and Yogi Berra plant Italian kisses on Hank Bauer after the decisive Game 6 of the 1951 World Series. Bauer socked a bases-loaded triple in the sixth inning of the 4-3 Yankees triumph. Right: After Bobby

Thomson's playoff-winning homer — and his astrologist's predictions — Giants manager Leo Durocher (left) felt good about his chances against Casey Stengel (right) and the Yankees.

uniform from six to five," recalled Durocher. "And she also told him to always wear something purple. Then she got to me. I was going to get off to the worst start I ever had . . . The first half of the season was going to be so bad, she said, that when I came up to my birthday we would be half a step from falling into last place . . . After my birthday, she said, things would change and I would go on to have the greatest season

on Bobby Thomson's legendary "Shot Heard 'Round the World" home run. The Giants' fate seemed in the stars, and Durocher began to believe in destiny. "It was like we were following a Hollywood script," he said.

Leo wasn't the only New Yorker who dreamed big in October 1951. Sky-high Giants fans hoped their team's momentum could carry them to their first world championship since 1933, while Yankees fans envisioned a third straight world title for manager Casey Stengel's club. Perhaps Thomson would play the hero one more time, or maybe the aging Joe DiMaggio would summon once last moment of glory. Then again, spectacular rookie center fielders Willie Mays and Mickey Mantle might prove heroic.

More than 65,000 fans turned out at Yankee Stadium for Game 1 of the Subway Series. The Giants pitching staff was so worn out after the Dodgers series that Durocher had to send No. 4 starter Dave Koslo to the hill. Yet the crafty southpaw defused the Bronx Bombers for nine innings, yielding just one run. Meanwhile, former Negro Leaguer Monte Irvin provided offensive fireworks, smacking three singles and a triple. His audacious steal of home in the first inning gave the Giants a 2-0 lead, and they prevailed 5-1.

Giants won 6-2, and Durocher couldn't wait to tell everyone about the middle-aged astrologer from Florida.

The woman, however, looked like she might be a fraud, as the Yankees won the next two games at the Polo Grounds. Starter Allie "Superchief" Reynolds, who had tossed two no-hitters during the 1951 regular season, handcuffed the Giants in Game 4, a 6-2 Yankees triumph. In Game 5, the trash-tossing Lopat again yielded one run over nine innings, this time prevailing 13-1. The score actually was tied 1-1 until the top of the third, when Yankees rookie Gil McDougald blasted a grand slam — only the third "grannie" ever clubbed in a World Series.

Prior to Game 6 at Yankee Stadium, Durocher submitted a disturbing letter he had received to MLB Commissioner Ford Frick. The author of the letter had offered the Giants manager a $15,000 bribe if he

Outfielder Monte Irvin sparked the Giants with a steal of home in the first inning of Game 1. The Giants won Games 1 and 3 but lost the last three battles.

The next day turned out miserably for both teams. Junkballer Eddie Lopat frustrated the Giants en route to a 3-1 victory. But when Mantle tripped on an exposed outfield sprinkler in the fifth inning, he twisted his knee so badly that he left the Series for good. Not only would he undergo surgery, but the injury would plague him the rest of his career, necessitating five more operations.

In the Polo Grounds in Game 3, second baseman Eddie Stanky came up big for the Giants. Attempting to steal on a pitchout in the fifth inning, Stanky looked to be dead meat at second base. Yet the "Brash Brat" kicked the ball out of shortstop Phil Rizzuto's glove. The play ignited a five-run rally, capped by a Whitey Lockman three-run homer. The

lost the remaining games of the Series. Leo had no intention of losing, of course, but he couldn't stop the Yankees' onslaught.

Game 6 was tied 1-1 in the sixth when burly ex-Marine Hank Bauer — one of the many platoon players employed by Stengel — brought 61,000 fans to their feet. With the bases full of future Hall of Famers (Yogi Berra, DiMaggio, and Johnny Mize), Bauer rocketed a drive to deep left center. The three runners scored, and Bauer rumbled into third with a triple.

The Yankees maintained their 4-1 lead entering the ninth, but it appeared the Giants might have one last miracle left in them. The top three men in the order — Stanky, Alvin Dark, and Whitey Lockman

— all singled to load the bases. Reliever Bob Kuzava entered for the Yankees, and Irvin tagged him with a fly-out that advanced all three runners.

Unbelievably, Thomson came to bat in the exact situation in which he had victimized the Dodgers with his historic shot: ninth inning, 4-2 score, runners on second and third, and one out. This time, though, Thomson managed only a sacrifice fly, making it a 4-3 game. Pinch hitter Sal Yvars looked like he might tie the score when he rifled a low liner to right. But Bauer, charging hard like he did in Okinawa during World War II, speared the ball just inches above the

Yankees rookie Gil McDougald broke open Game 5 with a grand slam in the third inning, fueling a 13-1 rout.

ground, concluding the series.

In the end, none of the glittering stars had come through in the fall classic. Mays batted just .182, Mantle mustered only one hit, and Thomson failed to repeat his heroics. Meanwhile, DiMaggio led World Series batters in strikeouts before announcing his retirement, saying "I'm not Joe DiMaggio anymore."

Durocher would forever enjoy telling his astrologer story, but the tale would always fizzle out at the end. No Hollywood script would ever be written about the 1951 fall classic, and in time it would be almost entirely overshadowed by Thomson's shot in the NL playoff. Yet several players did make this an exciting Series, and their efforts deserve to be remembered. Here's a tip of the cap to Koslo, Irvin, Stanky, McDougald, Lopat, and Bauer — unsung heroes of the "forgotten World Series."

CASEY'S PLATOON

Early in his career, Yankees phenom Mickey Mantle smashed the dugout's water supply after a particularly frustrating at-bat, to which manager Casey Stengel, nicknamed "The Ol' Perfesser," snapped, "It ain't the water cooler which is getting you out."

Upon taking over the reins of the Yankees in 1949, Stengel led the team to an MLB-record five consecutive world titles (1949-53). Many attribute their success to Stengel's managerial genius.

The retort about the water cooler was pure Stengel, reflecting his butchered English, his sense of humor, and his deft ability to use sarcasm to light a fire under his troops. Casey also stroked his players' egos at appropriate times, such as when he praised Mantle for having "more speed than any slugger and more slug than any speedster."

Stengel didn't seem real bright, but his instincts for the game were uncanny. "He made what some people call stupid moves," recalled pitcher Don Larsen, "but about eight or nine out of ten of them worked."

Stengel, who learned the game from legendary New York Giants manager John McGraw, mastered the art of platooning. He platooned not only because right-handed batters hit better off lefties (and vice versa), but for less obvious reasons. For instance, he shielded young hitters from crafty veteran pitchers. He also figured a regular would be fresher late in the season if he took 30 games off, and that a reserve would stay sharper if he played a lot. "If I know I'm gonna have to use both of them," he explained, "I might as well use each of them the best way."

Stengel platooned incessantly in 1951. Eleven Yankees played at least 96 games, but only two (All-Stars Phil Rizzuto and Yogi Berra) played more than 131. Their performance in the last three games of the World Series — outscoring the Giants 23-6 — proved how important it was to stay fresh.

CHAPTER 8

ONE FOR THE THUMB

1953 WORLD SERIES

September 30, 1953-October 5, 1953 — New York: It was hardly news that the Yankees were back in the Fall Classic in 1953. A World Series without the Yankees was like Christmas without Bing Crosby or summer without the beach.

Worldwide events reflected change in 1953. Nikita Khrushchev won a power struggle in the Soviet Union after the death of Joseph Stalin; convicted spies Julius and Ethel Rosenberg were executed; and an armistice in Korea was signed. U.S.

Bombers" to four straight World Series championships entering the 1953 Series. Their opponent would once again be their crosstown rival from the Senior Circuit, the Brooklyn Dodgers.

The Yankees' incredible run of four consecutive World Series championships began in 1949 during Stengel's first season as manager. A year earlier, the Yankees had finished in third place under Bucky Harris; that third place finish had been enough to get Harris fired and the colorful Stengel hired.

New York Yankees infielder Billy Martin gets a hug from coach Frank Crosetti (2) as his teammates celebrate their World Series championship at Yankee Stadium on Oct. 5, 1953. Martin's hit in last of ninth inning drove in the run that beat the Brooklyn Dodgers, 4-3, in the sixth and deciding Series game. The win gave the Yankees their fifth straight Series championship. From left are Irv Noren, Andy Carey, Martin, Crosetti, Jim McDonald, Bill Miller, and Ed Lopat (wearing cap).

Air Force test pilot Chuck Yeager set a speed record in an X-1 rocket plane — and an expedition led by Sir Edmund Hillary became the first to reach the summit of Mount Everest.

Meanwhile, the Yankees rolled on like a steamroller, a constant amid all the changes.

Casey Stengel had managed the "Bronx

Stengel arrived in New York with a reputation based more on his sense of humor than managerial acumen. He had enjoyed little success in previous stints as a major-league manager with the Dodgers and Braves. Nevertheless, under Stengel, the Yankees returned to the World Series in 1949 and defeated the Dodgers in five games.

More Yankees dominance followed. In 1950 the Yankees swept the Philadelphia Phillies to claim their second consecutive Series. They disposed of the New York Giants in six games in 1951. And thanks to Billy Martin's seventh-inning heroics in Game 7, the Yankees defeated the Dodgers in 1952 for their fourth straight world championship. With two outs and the bases loaded, the Yankees second baseman charged in from his position and fell to his knees to grab Jackie Robinson's pop fly — and kill a Dodgers' rally.

Yankees grabbed the momentum from the outset, when Martin hit a bases-loaded triple off Erskine to lead a four-run first inning. The Dodgers came back with homers by Jim Gilliam, Gil Hodges and George Shuba to tie the score at 5; Shuba's blast was the first pinch-hit home run by a National League player in World Series history. But Joe Collins hit a solo home run off Clem Labine in the seventh to put the Yankees up 6-5. The Yankees added three more in the eighth to take a 9-5 win.

Dodgers players rush to congratulate Carl Erskine, fourth from right, after he completed a brilliant pitching performance against the Yankees in the third game of the World Series at Ebbets Field, Brooklyn, October 2, 1953. Erskine held the Yankees to six hits, struck out 14 for a then-Series record, and won 3-2. Among the other Dodgers are Joe Black (49), Don Zimmer (9), Gil Hodges (14), Jackie Robinson (rear), and Pee Wee Reese (right).

In the span of the Yankees' four-year run, Stengel's stock rose immensely, to the point that he was hailed as a baseball genius. During this time, the Yankees bid goodbye to Joe DiMaggio, whose place in center field was taken by rising superstar, Mickey Mantle.

Many felt the Dodgers had improved enough in 1953 to finally defeat the Yankees in the World Series and claim their first world championship. Pitching provided the Dodgers' strong suit.

Carl Erskine led the Dodgers' rotation with a 20-win season and was backed up by Russ Meyer who won 15; Billy Loes had 14 wins to his credit and Preacher Roes had 11. Combined with a solid everyday lineup, the Dodgers of manager Charlie Dressen stormed to the National League pennant, taking the flag by 13 games over the Milwaukee Braves.

Whitey Ford's 18 wins led a Yankees roster that had finished first in the American League with a 2.43 ERA. And the Yankees had an everyday lineup boasting of Mantle, Martin, Yogi Berra, Hank Bauer and Phil Rizzuto.

Game 1 took place at Yankee Stadium, where the

Martin again made his presence known in Game 2 with a solo home run that tied the score at 2. Mantle put the game away in the eighth with a two-run homer to give the Yankees — and starter Eddie Lopat — a 4-2 lead over Roe, who had pitched well for the Dodgers.

The Series shifted to Ebbets Field for Game 3, where Erskine changed the momentum of the Series by striking out 14 — including Mantle, who struck out four times. Catcher Roy Campanella hit a solo home run in the eighth that broke a 2-2 tie for a 3-2 Dodgers win. Duke Snider had two doubles and a home run in Game 4 en route to a 7-3 Dodgers win that tied the Series at two games apiece. Still playing on the enemy turf of Ebbets Field for Game 5, Martin and Mantle led an 11-hit Yankees attack with home runs en route to an 11-7 Yankees victory.

The Series shifted back to Yankee Stadium for Game 6, where the Dodgers hoped to catch the proverbial lightning in a bottle by sending Erskine to the mound on two days' rest. Ford, who had lasted just one inning in Game 4, started for the Yankees.

With 62,370 fans packed into Yankee Stadium, the Yankees took a 3-0 lead in the first and carried a

3-1 lead into the ninth inning. Ford had allowed just one run in seven innings. Allie Reynolds took over to pitch a scoreless eighth before surrendering a game tying two-run homer to Carl Furillo in the ninth.

Unfortunately for the Dodgers, Martin had a turn at bat in the bottom half of the inning. Labine walked Baer to lead off the ninth before Mantle topped a one-out grounder that ricocheted off Billy Cox's glove at third to bring Martin to the plate.

Yankees outfielder Mickey Mantle connects with relief hurler Russ Meyer's first pitch in the third inning to smash a grand slam into the left center field stands in Game 5 of the World Series, October 4, 1953, at Ebbets Field in Brooklyn. Mantle's drive, just the fourth bases-filled home run in World Series history, helped the Yankees defeat the Dodgers, 11-7.

Martin had hit just .257 during the regular season, but he had been the spark for the Yankees throughout the Series, accruing 11 hits to that point. Martin worked the count to 1-1 before lacing a crisp single up the middle to score Bauer for a 4-3 Yankees win. The single established a record with 12 hits in a six-game World Series. In addition, Martin had eight RBI and a .500 average.

The Dodgers had lost in the Series for the seventh time in seven chances. Meanwhile, the Yankees had done it again, winning the World Series for a record fifth consecutive time.

Ironically, the Yankees won 100 games for the first time under Stengel the following season, but were dethroned by the Cleveland Indians, who won an incredible 111 games in 1954.

STENGEL'S PROTEGE

After the Series, New York Yankee Billy Martin has some fun in Honolulu.

Yankees manager Casey Stengel always had a soft spot for Billy Martin. Martin had limited skills but he knew how to play the game, had a spirited approach, and hungered to win — all traits that reminded Stengel of himself when he played the game. During his first season as manager of the Oakland Oaks in 1946, Stengel got his first glimpse of Martin, a high school student who played for the Junior Oaks in exhibitions before the regular games.

Stengel followed Martin's career and was instrumental in Martin being signed to a contract with a Yankees farm team in 1946. Stengel became manager of the Yankees in 1949. By the end of that season, the fiery second baseman was in the Yankees' infield. Once Martin arrived in the major leagues, he made his presence felt and the Yankees thrived.

In Martin's first four seasons as a Yankee, the team won four pennants and four world championships. When Martin served in the Army in 1954 the Yankees finished second to the Indians. When he returned in 1955, the Yankees won two more pennants and one World Series.

CHAPTER 9

THE GIANT UPSET

1954 WORLD SERIES

September 29-October 2, 1954 — Cleveland: The 1954 World Series brought a different flavor to the fall classic. Year after year, the New York Yankees had worn their regal pinstripes like black tie and tails, while their play made all other baseball players look like frustrated crooners in zoot suits.

But in 1954 the Cleveland Indians stepped to the forefront to bring about a decidedly different outcome to the American League pennant race — and thereby

getting older, but you could still see him winning 10 to 15 games and the same thing with Houtteman. I think that's the best staff I ever saw on any club."

The position players were an experienced and talented group led by third baseman Al Rosen. Still, beating the Yankees seemed to be as remote a prospect as scaling Mount Everest without a rope.

"I kind of got a kick out of the writers back then," Lopez said. "Red Smith and Frankie Graham were both

Left: The most famous catch in baseball history. Running at top speed, back to the plate, New York Giants center fielder Willie Mays catches up to a 450-foot blast from Cleveland's Vic Wertz. Mays pulled the ball down just in front of the bleacher wall in the eighth inning of the World Series opener at the Polo Grounds in New York.

September 29, 1954. Mays made the grab just one step from crashing into the wall. Right: Willie Mays was no stranger to spectacular plays. Here, he leaps high off the ground to rob Dodger center fielder Duke Snider of extra bases at Ebbets Field in Brooklyn, August 15, 1954.

changed the climate of the World Series.

Shortly before his death in 2005, former Indians manager Al Lopez reminisced about the season still fondly remembered on the banks of the Cuyahoga River. Lopez begins any conversations about the 1954 team by touting the starting staff of Bob Lemon, Early Wynn, Mike Garcia, Bob Feller and Art Houteman. All were experienced and talented.

"That was an All-Star staff," said Lopez, who was elected to baseball's Hall of Fame in 1977. "Imagine what a staff like that would be worth today. You knew right away that Lemon, Wynn and Garcia would be worth about 60 or so wins right off the bat. Feller was

real nice guys. They used to stay in St. Petersburg [covering the Yankees during the spring] and they'd come to Sarasota when we played [the Yankees]. They'd say, 'Well, Al, whadaya gonna do this year? You gonna beat the Yankees?' And I'd say yes. Then they'd laugh. After the 1954 season it was nice when I saw Red Smith and I finally got to hear him say, 'Well, you told me.'"

In the spring Lopez always told everyone who cared to listen that the Indians were going to win the pennant. Privately, however, he knew that the Yankees had more weapons than any other team in the league.

"The players liked [Yankees manager] Casey

[Stengel]," Lopez said, chuckling while remembering one of baseball's special characters. "And he had some great players with the Yankees, so he could try some unpredictable things. The reason he did? Confidence in his club. He could get away with doing unpredictable things with the talent he had on the team.

"I played for [Casey] at Boston and Brooklyn and he didn't try any of these unpredictable things. We just went out and tried to win in our simple way. I wasn't one of those unpredictable guys. I played percentages and I think in the long run it paid off."

Lopez called his team a "close-knit bunch of nice guys." "They were always pulling together," he said. "You'd think after the Yankees had beaten us every year they'd pack it in and expect to get beat. But that wasn't their way. I think a lot of the closeness stemmed from the fact we rode the train back then."

said. "With the Yankees coming to town to play a double-header on Sunday, I rotated the pitching staff so I'd have my best two pitchers against them, Wynn and Lemon. Sweeping that doubleheader put us up 7 games. That was about it."

Cleveland finished with a record-setting 111 wins in a 154-game season. Ironically, it was the first time one of Stengel's teams had surpassed 100 wins in a season with 103, but the Yankees still finished eight games behind the Indians.

With 10 days left in the season, the Indians clinched the pennant in advance of their World Series appearance against the New York Giants. Bobby Avila led the Indians and the American League with a .341 batting average, while teammate Larry Doby led the league in home runs with 32 and RBI with 126.

The Giants managed to win the National League pennant by five games to advance to the World Series,

The 1954 batting champions, Bobby Avila, left, of the American League pennant-winning Cleveland Indians, and Willie Mays, of the National League champions New York Giants, pose with their bats at the Polo Grounds in New York City prior to the World Series. Avila had a .341 average in 1954, while Mays ended the season at .345.

The Yankees went to Cleveland's Municipal Stadium on September12 for a Sunday double-header. An all-time record crowd of 86,563 showed for the twin bill and the Indians swept the American League's longtime bullies, 4-1 and 3-2.

"At the time we were 5 games out front," Lopez

where they appeared to be decided underdogs. For starters, the Giants had won 14 fewer games than the Indians during the regular season. And the team's pitching looked weak.

Game 1 was played September 29, 1954 at the Polo Grounds, the Giants' storied home field. In the eighth inning with the score tied at 2, Indians first baseman Vic Wertz hit a 450-foot blast to center field. In virtually any other park in the major leagues, Wertz's drive would have been a home run. At the Polo Grounds, however, Willie Mays ran down the ball to make a memorable over-the-shoulder catch.

"It was a great catch, there was no question about it," Lopez says. "If we'd have been playing in Cleveland, I think it would have gone over the fence. I think [Mays] overran it a little bit. But he had to run at top speed to deep centerfield. That was a tremendous catch."

The game had advanced to extra innings when Giants manager Leo Durocher decided to play a hunch by using Dusty Rhodes to pinch-hit for Monte Irvin. It was the 10th inning, with two runners aboard and the score still tied at 2. Indians right-hander Bob Lemon threw a high curve ball on the first pitch and Rhodes swung. He connected with the pitch and hit a drive that landed in the first row, approximately seven feet

Cleveland Indians manager Al Lopez tries to look the part of a tribal chieftain, wearing a headdress and letting out a war chant, before his club lost to the Giants 3-1 in the second game of the World Series at the Polo Grounds in New York City, September 30, 1954.

inside the right field foul line. The Giants had a 5-2 victory.

Lopez never forgot the cruel geometry of the Polo Grounds. "The longest out and the shortest home run of the season beat us," Lopez said.

Rhodes got a game-tying single and followed with a home run to lead a 3-1 Giants win in Game 2. Cleveland's Municipal Stadium hosted Game 3 and once again, Rhodes led the way with a critical single during a third-inning rally for a 6-2 Indians win. The following day, the Giants completed their sweep of the Indians with a 7-4 win.

"We had some kind of team," Lopez says. "Even though we lost the Series, I still think that was one of the best teams in baseball history."

LONGEST OUT OF THE SEASON

Baseball is an odd sport. It relies on statistics and numbers to tell its story more than any other sport, yet it is the only sport not to play on a uniform field. Yes, the distance from the pitchers mound to home plate is consistent, as is the distance around the bases. But the dimensions of the outfield vary from park to park, often making a mockery of should-be outcomes.

Nowhere was this more evident than Game 1 of the 1954 World Series played at the Polo Grounds, the home field of the New York Giants, who were playing the Cleveland Indians.

Center field at the Polo Grounds brought to mind a vast wilderness extending 483 feet from home plate, yet the right field line brought the most intimate distance in the major leagues: 270 feet from home plate to the foul pole. These distances ultimately worked against the Indians in their World Series bid.

In the eighth inning of Game 1, Vic Wertz hit a 450-foot drive to center field that Willie Mays ran down to make his famed over-the-shoulder catch. Had the game been in Cleveland's Municipal Stadium, the ball would have likely been a home run, which would have given the Indians a win.

When the game went into the 10th inning, Giants pinch hitter Dusty Rhodes homered right down the right field line — the cheapest home run in baseball — for a game winner that would have been an out in Cleveland.

Until his death in 2005, Cleveland manager Al Lopez remained frustrated in a "dad gummit," good-natured, sort of way. As he so aptly put it, "The longest out and the shortest home run of the season beat us."

CHAPTER 10

THE BOYS OF SUMMER

1955 WORLD SERIES

October 4, 1955 — New York: On one of baseball's most magical afternoons, "Dem Bums" finally shed their hard-luck label and became forever known as the "Boys of Summer." It was a long time coming, to be sure. The Brooklyn Dodgers, talented enough to reach the World Series four times between 1947 and 1953, were never quite good enough to be called the best team in their town.

That distinction belonged wholly to the New York Yankees, who beat the Dodgers in all four of those World Series and won six titles in the same seven-year span from 1947 to 1953, including four in a row under manager Casey Stengel beginning in 1949. One might have called Brooklyn the Bronx Bombers' crosstown rival, but a rivalry implies competitiveness. And when it came to their almost annual World Series meetings, the results spoke for themselves.

Led by the likes of Joe DiMaggio, Mickey Mantle, Tommy Henrich and Billy Martin, the Yankees took the Dodgers in seven games in 1947, five games in 1949, seven games in 1952 and six games in 1953. Rooting for Brooklyn meant developing an intense hatred for the club's National League rival, the New York Giants. The Series losses to the Yankees, however, produced something more akin to loathing toward the Bronx Bombers on the part of Dodger fans.

There was an aura of invincibility surrounding the Yankees, and no one knew it better than Dem

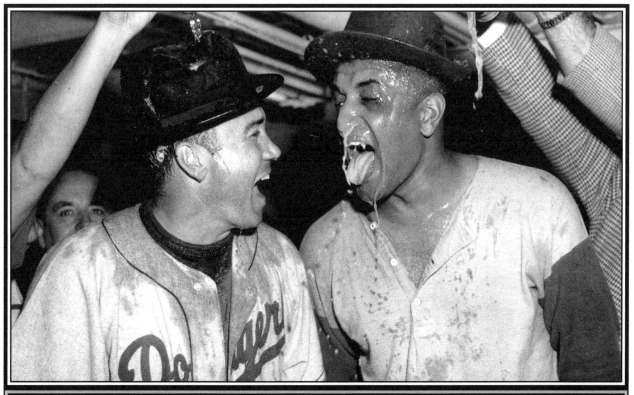

Brooklyn Dodgers center fielder Duke Snider, left, and pitcher Don Newcombe wear hats filled with beer as they celebrate in the dressing room after winning the 1955 World Series. The clinching seventh game took place at Yankee Stadium in New York City on Oct. 4, 1955. Newcombe was 0-1 in the Series after a 20-5 regular season, but Snider hit four home runs in the fall classic.

Bums. A *Brooklyn Eagle* editorial in 1952 speculated that "Maybe the Yankees are professional World Series players. Perhaps … they cast a spell over the opponents and give them the jitters before the battle gets fairly under way. But there comes a day …"

To the delight of Brooklyn fans, that day finally arrived in 1955. As teenagers across America were grooving to a song credited with kicking off the rock-n-roll era — Bill Haley and the Comets' "Rock Around the Clock" — the Dodgers were dancing circles around their National League foes and setting up yet another World Series struggle with the hated Yankees.

Pitching ace Don Newcombe won 20 games against five losses in 1955. Star center fielder Duke Snider batted .309 with 42 home runs and 136 RBI. Catcher Roy Campanella added a .318 average and 32 long balls. Pee Wee Reese, Jackie Robinson, Carl Furillo and Gil Hodges also helped deliver another National League pennant by a 13 1/2-game margin over Milwaukee.

Their fifth World Series date in nine years started in predictable fashion. New York took the

The usual 64,000-plus fans packed Yankee Stadium for the final two games of the set. The first of those — a 5-1 New York victory — assured a deciding game that figured to go the Yankees' way. After all, the home team had won all six games to that point. After all, these were the Brooklyn Dodgers. As Stengel had told reporters, "Don't worry. The Yankees always take care of the Series."

Brooklyn manager Walter Alston sent Podres back to the mound for the finale, against Game 2 winner Tommy Byrne. Baseball legend holds that Podres told his teammates before the game that if they gave him one run, he would take care of the rest. Podres could not recall actually saying that in later years, but his teammates agreed that his

Brooklyn lefty Johnny Podres pitched two complete-game victories in the 1955 World Series, allowing just one earned run in 18 innings. He won Game 3 8-3 and gutted out a tough 2-0 win in the deciding Game 7. Podres won 148 games in a 15-year major-league career.

first two games at Yankee Stadium; now all they needed was just one victory at Ebbets Field over the next three days to put a virtual stranglehold on another world title. Even the most optimistic Brooklynites had to be thinking, "Here we go again."

The Dodgers' Robinson summed up what was at stake, saying, "We gotta win this one. If we lose again, they'll be calling us choke-up guys the rest of our lives. Do we want that?"

At Ebbets Field, the tide turned. Johnny Podres pitched the Dodgers to an 8-3 victory on his 23rd birthday, and Campanella homered for the second straight day in Game 4, an 8-5 Brooklyn romp. The Dodgers then made it three home wins in a row in a 5-3 nail-biter behind Snider's pair of home runs.

confidence set the tone for the game.

The Dodgers produced that one run in the fourth inning, when Campanella doubled and scored on a single by Hodges. Aided by a Yankee error, Hodges drove in a second run in the sixth inning when his sacrifice fly sent Reese across home plate.

Pitching with the hopes of a franchise and its long-suffering fans on his shoulders, Podres was brilliant. He did run into trouble in the sixth inning, but was rescued by one of the greatest catches in World Series history. With two men on and nobody out, Yogi Berra drove what looked like an extra-base hit toward the left field corner, but speedy outfielder Sandy Amoros raced toward it, stretched out his glove and made the grab near the stands. He fired to shortstop Reese, whose relay to first base narrowly doubled up runner Gil McDougald.

The Yankees never recovered. The final out came when Elston Howard grounded to shortstop. Reese fired a low throw to first, but Hodges reached and made the catch that sent the Dodgers racing onto the field to celebrate their first world title. Tears streamed down the faces of their fans, many of whom left their homes, boarded the subway and headed for Flatbush Avenue to toast their victorious underdogs.

"That win," said pitcher Carl Erskine, "meant we finally brought respect to the borough of Brooklyn. Did we celebrate? It never stopped."

Brooklyn fans woke up the next morning to a

Sandy Amoros, just inserted into the game as a defensive replacement, makes a tremendous running catch off a Yogi Berra line drive in the sixth inning of Game 7 of the 1955 World Series. Amoros' catch helped clinch the Dodgers' 2-0 win and bring Brooklyn its first World Championship.

changed existence. Life was good. Two new kids' television shows debuted that day — Captain Kangaroo and The Mickey Mouse Club. The Dodgers had shattered the invincibility of their despised crosstown rival. Dem Bums were World Series champions for the first time.

Those fans had no idea how quickly their party would end. The Dodgers lost in six games to the Yankees in the 1956 World Series. And the following year, owner Walter O'Malley announced that the team was moving to Los Angeles for the 1958 season. But no one could ever take that one magical season from the Boys of Summer.

WILLIE, MICKEY, AND THE DUKE

"Who's the best center fielder in New York?" It was an oft-asked question among baseball fans in the 1950s, and there was no clear-cut right answer among the three choices. Willie Mays patrolled center for the New York Giants. Not only had he won the National League MVP Award and led the Giants to a 1954 World Series title, but no one could match the genuine exuberance of the "Say Hey Kid."

Mickey Mantle was "The Mick" among Yankee fans. The fun-loving slugger captured the American League Triple Crown and MVP Award in 1956 and added a second MVP the following year. More important, he powered the Bronx Bombers to a remarkable run of team success, leading them to five World Series championships in the 1950s. For a larger-than-life persona and tape-measure home runs, Mantle was in a league of his own.

Then there was "The Duke." Though clearly deserving to be mentioned in such company, the Dodgers' Edwin Donald "Duke" Snider tended to take a backseat to the other two. His numbers were steady across the board — he finished among the top three in most National League batting categories at one time or another — but he rarely put up gargantuan statistics in any particular category to grab the kind of attention Mays and Mantle could command. His often-stormy relationship with the press did not help Snider's cause, either.

When Brooklyn's Boys of Summer ended their championship drought in 1955, however, Snider finally got his due. He had long been a favorite among Dodger fans, but now that his strong arm, powerful bat (.320 with four home runs and an .840 slugging average in the World Series) and leadership had won them a title, the "Lord of Flatbush" was once and for all a New York, and baseball, legend.

Willie, Mickey and the Duke: an unparalleled one-town trio.

CHAPTER 11

HAMMER TIME

1957 WORLD SERIES

October 2-10, 1957 — New York: Henry Aaron wasn't a household name when the 1957 season opened. He lacked excitement, which added to his grace as a ballplayer in the minds of some, while others thought he appeared lazy and complacent — which he was neither. Opponents knew as much.

During a Braves-Dodgers contest early in Aaron's career, all-time great Jackie Robinson was stationed at third base for the Dodgers and showed

play baseball in high school. He instead played semipro baseball beginning at the age of 15 and went on to become a shortstop at age 18 for the Negro Leagues' Indianapolis Clowns; Aaron played two seasons for the Clowns before the Braves purchased his contract for $7,500. After a season and a half, he became the first African-American player to join the Braves in 1954. That year — the Braves' second season in Milwaukee — Aaron took

American League Most Valuable Player Mickey Mantle of the Yankees, left, and his National League counterpart, Hank Aaron of the Milwaukee Braves, cross bats at Yankee Stadium, May 12, 1958. The two played against each other in the 1957 and 1958 World Series, but no title was at stake that day, as the Yankees and Braves played a charity game to benefit sandlot baseball and cancer research for children.

no interest when Aaron feigned a bunt on two occasions. Puzzled about why a great ballplayer such as Robinson would choose such a tactic, Aaron asked Robinson about it afterward. Robinson replied, "We'll give you first base anytime you want it."

Aaron grew up in Mobile, Alabama, but did not

over Bobby Thomson's place in left field after Thomson broke his ankle in spring training.

"Hammerin' Hank" hit .280 with 13 home runs as a 160-pound rookie during his rookie season, which ended when he broke his ankle in September of 1954. Aaron moved to right field in 1955 and won the National League batting title in 1956 when he hit .328, complemented by 28 home runs. Aaron's NL batting title set the stage for 1957, when his understated style finally commanded the attention of all baseball fans.

Aaron had seasoned well by 1957, packing 180 pounds on his lean, powerful frame. The added strength and weight served Aaron well and, seemingly, he could do no wrong en route to a near Triple Crown. He led the National League in home runs with 44, RBI with 132 and runs scored with 118, but finished tied for third with Frank Robinson in batting average at .322 — behind Stan Musial (.351) and Willie Mays (.333). Aaron might have had a better chance at winning the batting title as well, but he was nagged by an ankle injury that he'd suffered from stepping on a bottle thrown onto the field.

Among the highlights of Aaron's memorable 1957 season was a game against the Dodgers on Aug. 24, 1957, when he hit the first grand slam of his career in a 13-7 win. But Aaron's personal favorite came Sept. 23, 1957, when he hit a game-winning home run against the St. Louis Cardinals in the 11th inning to clinch the pennant for the Braves.

While Aaron's contribution to the Braves in 1957 was immense, the Braves hardly were a one-man show. Managed by Fred Haney, the Braves had a lineup featuring Eddie Mathews, Del Crandall and Red Schoendienst; pitchers included Warren Spahn, who led the team with 21 wins, Lew Burdette and Bob Buhl. But was this compilation of players enough to defeat the powerful New York Yankees?

Under manager Casey Stengel, the Yankees had won eight American League pennants during his nine-year tenure. Wearing the Yankees pinstripes was the usual cast of heroes, led by Mickey Mantle, Yogi Berra, Bill Skowron, and Whitey Ford.

The World Series opened on Oct. 2, 1957, in

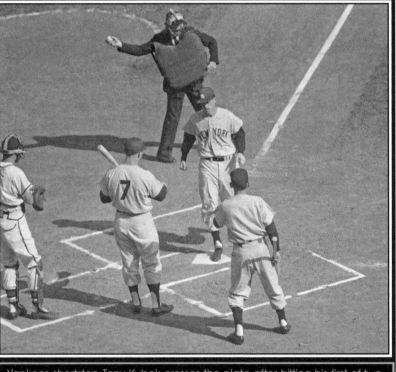

Yankees shortstop Tony Kubek crosses the plate after hitting his first of two home runs in Game 3 of the 1957 World Series in Milwaukee, a game the Yankees won 12-3. Milwaukee native Kubek, just 21, had only three homers in the regular season.

New York and Ford took a 3-1 decision over Spahn. The following day Burdette answered the call in Game 2 when he kept the Yankees off balance for nine innings by allowing just two runs on seven hits. The Braves won Game 2, 4-2.

In the first game played in Milwaukee, Don Larsen gave the Yankees 7 1/3 innings of quality relief pitching in Game 3 to help lead a 12-3 Yankees route. While the hometown team was crazy about the Braves, they also felt a great allegiance to the hometown boy, Tony Kubek. The Yankees rookie utility man was a native of Milwaukee and had two home runs and four RBI during the victory.

After what might have been a devastating loss, the Braves showed great resiliency at this point. Aaron and Frank Torre hit two-run homers to stake the Braves to a 4-1 lead in Game 4. With Spahn on the mound the Braves looked like they were home free until Elston Howard hit a two-out, three-run homer off Spahn in the ninth to tie the game.

The Yankees scored in the top of the 10th to take a 5-4 lead and set up one of the more memorable moments in major-league history. Pinch hitter Nippy Jones convinced home plate umpire Augie Donatelli that he'd been hit by a pitch by showing Donatelli a shoe polish stain on the baseball. Johnny Logan then doubled home pinch runner Felix Mantilla to tie the score. Mathews finished it off with a two-run homer to give the Braves a 7-5 win.

Burdette took the mound in Game 5 and pitched a complete-game gem against a Yankees lineup that did not include Mantle, who sat due to a sore shoulder. Mathews beat out an infield hit in the sixth inning against Ford and scored when Joe Adcock singled him home for the only run of the game. Burdette allowed no runs on seven hits to pick up his second win of the Series.

The Series returned to Yankee Stadium for Game 6 and Bob Turley pitched a four-hitter in a 3-2 Yankees win to force a seventh game.

Haney penciled in Spahn's name to start Game 7, but the left-hander came down with the flu and win also gave the Braves their first World Championship since 1914.

Aaron, who batted .393 with three homers and seven RBI during the Series, was named the National League's Most Valuable Player for 1957. He would go on to average 33 home runs a year

The key play of Game 4 of the 1957 World Series. Leading off the bottom of the tenth with his club down 5-4, Braves pinch hitter Nippy Jones shows plate umpire Augie Donatelli a smudge of shoe polish on the ball, proving that he was hit by Tommy Byrne's pitch. The invigorated Braves rallied for three runs to win the game, with Eddie Mathews' two-run homer the clincher.

Burdette took the ball with two days of rest. Aaron's RBI single highlighted a four-run third inning while Burdette gave the Yankees all they could handle for a third time. He pitched a complete-game seven-hit shutout to give Burdette his third complete-game victory of the Series. The and drive in more than 100 runs 15 times — including a record 13 seasons in a row. An All-Star in each of the 23 seasons he played, Aaron broke Babe Ruth's career home run mark in 1974. But 1957 would be the only season for which Aaron was honored as the league MVP.

CHAPTER 12

CALIFORNIA DREAMIN'

1959 WORLD SERIES

October 1-8, 1959 — Chicago: During spring training, Dutch psychic Peter Hurkos toured the National League camps on an assignment for *Parade* magazine. Hurkos admitted that he knew very little about baseball, but he anointed the Milwaukee Braves, the two-time defending champions, as the best team in the league.

Hurkos also said, however, that the Braves would not win the pennant. The man who had helped solve the Boston Strangler murders further predicted that the Giants would lead the NL for much of the year.

Spokane during the season when Dodgers general manager Buzzy Bavasi telephoned scout Red Corriden, who had discovered Sherry, and asked if he thought Sherry was ready for the major leagues. Based solely on Corriden's recommendation, Sherry was promoted. He lost two close games, then won seven in a row — helping the Dodgers tie Milwaukee and forcing a three-game playoff for the pennant.

In the playoff opener in Milwaukee, Sherry relieved in the second inning and kept the Braves scoreless, scattering four hits the rest of the game, as

The largest crowd ever to see a major-league game gathered in the Los Angeles Coliseum (above) on October 6, 1959. 92,706 fans attended Game 5 of the World Series between the Los Angeles Dodgers and the Chicago White Sox, which Chicago won 1-0.

But it would be the Los Angeles Dodgers, the seventh-place team in the league in 1958, who would rally to win the pennant during the last week of the season.

Few people gave Hurkos' predictions much credence, but perhaps he knew more about what the addition of Larry Sherry would mean to the Dodgers than many longtime baseball observers.

The 24-year-old Sherry was pitching at Triple-A

the Dodgers won 3-2. Yet amidst the celebrating, there was tragedy. During the eighth inning, while watching on television, Corriden had collapsed and died of a heart attack.

When the Dodgers won again the following day, Hurkos' preseason prediction had come true — they were in the World Series, facing Bill Veeck's Chicago White Sox. For the first time since 1919, Chicago had won the pennant by snapping the Yankees' four-year domination of the AL.

Led by their double-play combination of Luis Aparicio and Nellie Fox, the White Sox were a team built on pitching and defense. They finished sixth in the eight-team league in runs scored, but the "Go-Go Sox," as they were known, stole 113 bases — almost double the total of the next highest team in the league. Aparicio led the AL with 56 steals, more than the team total of six of the other seven teams.

All of baseball was surprised when the White Sox erupted for 11 runs to win the Series' opener, 11-0. The Dodgers remained confident, however, and when Sherry came out of the bullpen and clinched a 4-3 victory the following day, the Series was even at a game each as the teams headed to Los Angeles.

Game 3 was historic — the first World Series game played west of St. Louis — and an all-time

The White Sox pounded out 12 hits, but could only score one run, leaving 17 runners on base. Sherry again came out of the bullpen and struck out the side in the ninth, saving a 3-1 Los Angeles win.

In the fourth game, an eighth-inning homer by Gil Hodges broke a 4-4 tie. And once more, Sherry closed the door in the ninth, retiring the White Sox to bring the Dodgers within one win of the World Championship.

An even larger crowd than had witnessed Game 3 — 92,706 — packed the Coliseum for the fifth game, hoping the Dodgers would give them a reason to celebrate. The White Sox, however, finally found a way to keep Sherry out of the game, as Bob Shaw out dueled Sandy Koufax in a 1-0 victory that sent the Series back to Chicago.

Wasting little time in Game 6, the Dodgers pounded 39-year-old starter Early Wynn. They

Los Angeles Dodgers pitcher Larry Sherry, the 1959 World Series MVP (left), and center fielder Duke Snider embrace in the dressing room after defeating the Chicago White Sox 9-3 to win the World Series in game six at Comiskey Park in Chicago on Oct. 8, 1959.

record crowd of 92,394 fans jammed into the Los Angeles Coliseum. Originally built to host the 1932 Olympics, the Los Angeles Coliseum had been converted into a temporary home for the Dodgers while their new baseball-only park was being built. The right field fence stood 440 feet away from home plate, while the left field fence was so close, 251 feet, that a 40-foot screen was erected above the wall.

erupted for eight runs in the first four innings, including Duke Snider's NL-record 11th World Series home run. When Johnny Podres surrendered a three-run homer to Ted Kluszewski, his third of the Series, in the bottom of the fourth, Dodgers manager Walter Alston once more summoned Sherry from the bullpen.

Back on the pitcher's mound, Sherry proved that Corriden had been right to recommend him for the majors. Sherry allowed just four hits over the final 5 2/3 innings to score a 9-3 victory for the Dodgers, who won the World Series just two seasons after leaving Brooklyn for Los Angeles.

The win came on the same day that Charles Van Doren, a Columbia University professor who'd won a fortune on the game show *Twenty-One*, was fired by NBC-TV amid a Congressional investigation into the fixing of television game shows. A House panel was looking into allegations that Van Doren and other contestants had been provided with the correct answers to questions before episodes of *Twenty-One* were broadcast.

There was no investigation, however, into Hurkos' baseball predictions, which had turned out to be correct, primarily because of Sherry's performance.

Everybody who had watched the Series could have predicted that Sherry would be named the Most

First baseman Ted Kluszewski of the Chicago White Sox slugs a home run in Game 1 of the World Series at Chicago's Comiskey Park on October 1, 1959. During the regular season, Kluszewski hit just two home runs for the Sox, but hit three in the Series.

Valuable Player in the Series. He pitched in four of the six games, winning two and saving the other two Los Angeles wins. He allowed just one run in 12 2/3 innings — an ERA of 0.71.

The 1959 team was one of six NL championship clubs that Alston would manage in his career in Los Angeles, and it remained his favorite.

"They may not have had as much talent as others, but they had tremendous desire," Alston wrote in his autobiography. "They played like a championship team all the way. They were a manager's dream team."

And a psychic's.

TIPS FOR WATCHING THE WORLD SERIES

Because a World Series game had never been played in Los Angeles before, the local chapter of the Red Cross issued a set of 10 recommendations for fans going to the games. The list was entitled "The Care and Welfare of Dodger fans during a World Series."

For men, the Red Cross recommended:

1. Control your temper. White Sox fans sometimes hit back.
2. Don't flail about during moments of exultation; you may hit another Dodger fan.
3. During dropped third strikes or White Sox grand slam homers, lower your head quickly between your knees to avoid fainting.
4. Be sure your mouth is empty when cheering; those in front of you will appreciate it.
5. Sit with your own kind. If you sit among the enemy you may spend half your time planning to slug that guy yapping at Drysdale.
6. Watch those hot dogs; chomped-on fingers may taste all right but they don't feel so good.

For women, the recommendations were:

1. Don't wear high heels; it will be easier on your escort's instep if you are given to frenzied behavior.
2. Leave your hat at home. If you must wear one, make it a beret or beanie; much easier and safer to tear off and throw during moments of frustration.
3. Don't cheer too enthusiastically if you are encased in one of those whalebone things. If shapeliness is important, try the flexible kind; strangling your emotions isn't healthy.
4. Don't apply makeup during moments when those sitting around you are reaching for foul balls, unless your lipstick happens to be the tasty kind and digestible.

CHAPTER 13

MAZ'S MIGHTY BLAST

1960 WORLD SERIES, GAME 7

Top: Pittsburgh catcher Hal Smith is greeted by teammates Dick Groat (24) and Roberto Clemente (21) after hitting a three-run homer in the eighth inning of Game 7 of the 1960 World Series. The blast put the Pirates up 9-7 in a game some have called the greatest ever played. Bottom: Pittsburgh second baseman Bill Mazeroski, one of few players elected to the Hall of Fame almost entirely for his amazing glovework — and one very famous home run.

October 13, 1960 — Pittsburgh: Pardon New Yorkers if they felt a bit smug on the eve of the 1960 World Series. In the "town that never sleeps"— the home of Times Square, Broadway shows, and Madison Avenue glitz — the star-studded Yankees had put together a 15-game winning streak and cruised to their 10th American League pennant in 12 years.

Meanwhile, the opposing city in the World Series, Pittsburgh, was a town that slept a lot. After a long day of back-breaking labor in Pittsburgh's steel mills, workers trudged home for a much-needed shower, a full meal, and hopefully eight hard hours of slumber.

Like Pittsburgh's citizenry, the Pirates were a low-profile bunch. The team hadn't won a pennant in 33 years, and they spent most of the 1950s looking up from the cellar. No one on the 1960 club scored or drove in 100 runs, and they fielded players with straightforward names: Don Hoak, Dick Groat, and four other starters named Bill or Bob. Yet by scrapping for runs, playing hard-nosed defense, and getting gutsy pitching, the Pirates won 95 games to earn their trip to the fall classic.

Second baseman Bill "Maz" Mazeroski epitomized the Pirates. The clean-cut son of a coal miner, he simply got the job done — especially on defense, where he used an old, beat-up mitt. Teammate Roberto Clemente once found the ripped, patched-together glove on the field and tossed it into the stands. A kid took one look at it and threw it back.

The city of Pittsburgh prepared for Game 1 at Forbes Field with small-town charm. Pennsylvania Governor David Lawrence threw out the first pitch, and the University of Pittsburgh marching band accompanied local singer Billy Eckstine in the playing of the national anthem. The city was so excited that a local judge postponed the start of a murder trial so that a jury wouldn't be distracted by the series action.

Fittingly, Mazeroski played the hero in Game 1, as his two-run homer keyed a 6-4 Pirates victory. Beginning in Game 2, however, the series turned into a frenzied roller coaster ride.

Opposite: Fans and players rush toward home plate, awaiting Pittsburgh Pirates second baseman Bill Mazeroski, who has just clubbed a ninth-inning walk-off home run to win the World Series in Pittsburgh on Oct. 13, 1960. The Pirates won a thrilling best-of-seven set against the favored New York Yankees.

Whitey Ford, New York Yankees southpaw, is shown in action against the Pittsburgh Pirates in the third World Series game at Yankee Stadium in the Bronx, N.Y., Oct. 8, 1960. Ford and the Yankees won the game 10-0, but Pittsburgh went on to capture the Series.

The powerful Yankees offense erupted for 16 runs in Game 2, due in part to two home runs by superstar Mickey Mantle. New York pitcher Whitey Ford tossed a 10-0 shutout in Game 3 at Yankee Stadium, as Mantle went deep again, and all-American boy Bobby Richardson drove in six runs. The Pirates toughed out a 3-2 win in the fourth game, as bespectacled Bill Virdon spanked a two-run single. Maz came through again in Game 5, doubling in two runs in a 5-2 Pirates victory.

Facing elimination, the Yankees roared back in Game 6, pounding out 17 hits and plating 12 runs. The crafty Ford tossed his second shutout of the series, and through six games the Bombers had outscored the Pirates 46-17. A crowd of 36,683 packed the intimate Forbes Field for the decisive Game 7. Some predicted another Yankees blowout, but it turned out to be one of the most tension-packed games ever played.

Getting a rare start at first base, Pittsburgh's Rocky Nelson belted a two-run homer in the first. The Pirates led 4-0 through four innings before the Yankees came alive. Bill Skowron's fifth-inning homer closed the gap to 4-1, and a long, three-run bomb by Yogi Berra in the sixth made it 5-4 New York. The Yankees stretched the lead to 7-4 in the eighth on a Clete Boyer double.

With a man on first in the bottom of the eighth, Virdon hit an apparent double-play grounder to shortstop Tony Kubek. Yet the ball hit a pebble and

SNEAKING INTO THE HALL OF FAME

Over the years, Hall of Fame balloters have made it clear that they won't vote for a player based on one great season or a single historic moment. Don Larsen, Bobby Thomson, and Roger Maris — none of them are in the Hall of Fame. Bill Mazeroski, however, is a different case. An eight-time Gold Glover but a mediocre hitter, Maz likely would have fallen short of induction, but his epic blast in the 1960 World Series earned him special consideration.

Mazeroski was so adept at second base that players at the 1958 All-Star Game stopped what they were doing to watch him take fielding practice. Maz turned double plays in a blink of an eye, and his 1,706 career DPs remains a record for a middle infielder. However, his unimpressive offensive statistics — .260 career batting mark and averages of eight homers and 26 walks per season — convinced baseball writers not to send him to the Hall. In 2001, however, the Veterans Committee voted him in.

On August 5, 2001, Mazeroski brought a 12-page speech to the induction ceremony, but he was so overwhelmed with emotion that he cut himself short. "I don't think I'm gonna make it," he said. "I think you can kiss these 12 pages down the drain. I just want to thank everybody. I want to thank the Hall of Fame, I want to thank the Veterans Committee, I want to thank all the friends and family that made this long trip up here to listen to me speak and hear this crap. Thank you very, very much. Thanks everybody. That's enough."

bounced off Kubek's throat — a sign, perhaps, that God, too, had grown tired of the Yankees dynasty. Groat followed with a single to make it 7-5. Two outs later, with men on second and third, Clemente hit what seemed like an inning-ending chopper to first baseman Skowron — but he beat it out when pitcher Jim Coates failed to cover first. A run scored, making it 7-6 New York. The next batter, second-string catcher Hal Smith, belted a three-run homer to left. Fans went wild, as the Pirates now led 9-7.

Pittsburgh's Bob Friend, 0-2 as a starter in the series, came on in relief in the ninth inning. The reliever Ralph Terry opened with a high fastball for ball one. He threw another high heater, but this time Maz took a mighty rip — blasting one deep to left. Outfielder Yogi Berra drifted back and watched it sail into the trees beyond the wall. Incredibly, the coal miner's son had just become the first man ever to end the World Series with a walk-off home run.

As Maz danced around the bases, waving his helmet, fans poured onto the field, chasing their hero as he rounded third base. Across the city, drivers pounded their horns while office workers tossed ticker tape out the windows. For the first time since 1925,

Pittsburgh Pirates center fielder Bill Virdon makes a spectacular catch of Bob Cerv's deep drive in the seventh inning of Game 4 of the World Series on October 9, 1960, at Yankee Stadium. Rushing to assist is Roberto Clemente (21). Virdon's play helped preserve a 3-2 Pittsburgh victory.

Yankees tagged him again with two singles. In came Harvey Haddix, who retired Roger Maris but surrendered a run-scoring single to Mantle. With men on first and third and one out, Berra smashed a hard one-hopper to first that Nelson snared in dramatic fashion. He stepped on first for the second out and fired to second for a potential series-ending tag-out of Mantle. Yet the Mick, thinking quickly, scrambled back to first, allowing pinch runner Gil McDougald to score. It was all knotted up, 9-9.

Their nerves frayed, Pirates fans hoped Mazeroski could spark a rally in the bottom of the ninth. New

Pittsburgh fans knew what it was like to be world champions.

Though Forbes Field was torn down years ago, tributes to the fabled 1960 Pirates remain. The outfield walls still stand, and a Little League diamond — named Bill Mazeroski Field — sits behind the left field wall. Each year on October 13, a cadre of old-time Pirates fans gather at the remains of old Forbes. They listen to the broadcast of Game 7 of the 1960 World Series, reveling in what they rightfully could claim as the greatest game in the history of baseball.

CHAPTER 14

A GIANT SCARE

1962 WORLD SERIES, GAME 7

Top: New York Yankees second baseman Bobby Richardson hit just .148 in the 1962 World Series against the San Francisco Giants, but made the big defensive play to end the deciding Game 7. Bottom: Willie McCovey of the San Francisco Giants celebrates a two-run homer in Game 2 of the World Series against the New York Yankees at San Francisco's Candlestick Park on October 5, 1962. The fearsome McCovey was on the wrong end of the stick in Game 7 as his sharp line drive, caught by Yankees second baseman Bobby Richardson, ended the Series.

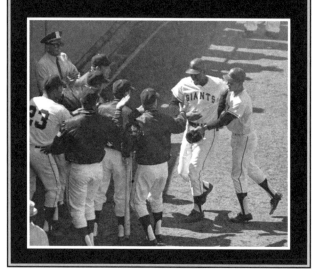

October 16, 1962 — San Francisco: Rain had soaked Candlestick Park for three successive days. The winds whipping off the Pacific coast helped dry the saturated ground enough that Game 7 of the World Series would be played, but it would be "one of those days" for the Yankees and Giants outfielders. Every fly ball was eligible to become an adventure.

On the East Coast, weather was the last thing on President John F. Kennedy's mind on this day. He had just received intelligence — photos taken by a U-2 reconnaissance aircraft and processed by the Central Intelligence Agency late the previous night — identifying Soviet nuclear missile installations under construction on Cuba, just 90 miles from the Florida coast.

Having learned of the missiles over breakfast, President Kennedy scheduled a meeting with his Executive Committee to discuss what measures the United States would take. The Cuban Missile Crisis had begun. Before hearing of this internationally critical series of events, however, Americans did what they always did in October. They tracked the World Series. And on this day, the participants treated them to what Yankees catcher Yogi Berra called the most exciting seventh game of a World Series he had ever witnessed.

Yankee starter Ralph Terry already held a place in World Series lore. Two years earlier, it was his pitch that Pittsburgh's Bill Mazeroski had turned into the most dramatic home run in World Series history, a ninth-inning, Game 7 blast that kept New York from giving manager Casey Stengel one last championship. Terry was responsible for the Yankees' only loss of the 1961 Series as well, but had accumulated 23 wins in 1962 and had been a complete-game victor in this set's Game 5.

The three consecutive rainouts allowed Yankee skipper Ralph Houk to come back with Terry in the deciding battle. He would be opposed by 24-game winner Jack Sanford, who also had pitched in Game 5 after shutting out the Yankees on three hits in the second game. The loser in that contest: Terry.

Nothing helps drama like a long buildup, and this Game 7 certainly had it. The three washouts in San

Opposite: Yankees pitcher Ralph Terry is carried off the field on his teammates' shoulders after winning the deciding Game 7 of the 1962 World Series at San Francisco's Candlestick Park on October 16, 1962. This would be the Yankees' last World Series triumph until 1977.

Ralph Terry, victorious in two 1962 World Series games, celebrates the Series-clinching Game 7 1-0 win by tossing his glove high into the air. The Series capped off a year in which Terry had won 23 games in the regular season.

AN AUTUMN OF CHANGE

Not everyone's attention was on baseball in the fall of 1962, though that year's World Series proved to be one of the most dramatic and riveting in history. At the same time the Yankees were holding off the Giants, President Kennedy was leading the United States through one of the most tumultuous and politically charged Octobers the nation has ever experienced. Much of it began even before the Cuban Missile Crisis.

The last day of September saw the President federalize the Mississippi National Guard and address Americans on live television regarding riots at the University of Mississippi, where James Meredith was trying to enroll as the first African-American student. The unrest was quelled on October 1, but not before 5,000 soldiers were pressed into action. Meanwhile, the U.S. government was stocking 36,000 public buildings with food, water and provisions in anticipation of using them as civil defense shelters.

There were some terrific national and international milestones between the Ole Miss rioting and the Cuban Missile Crisis, too. Johnny Carson took over as host of *The Tonight Show*, American astronaut Wally Schirra orbited the earth six times, the Second Ecumenical Council (Vatican II) convened in Rome and the Beatles released their first hit, "Love Me Do."

However, it was the Cuban Missile Crisis that pushed a nation's nerves to the brink.

October 22 — On national television, President Kennedy announced plans for a naval blockade of Cuba.

October 23 — The Soviets stated that the U.S. embargo of Cuba sets up the possibility of thermonuclear war.

October 24 — Soviet ships reached the quarantine line, but received orders from Moscow to hold their positions.

October 25 — U.S. Military Alert was set to DEFCON 2, the highest level in history.

October 26 — Soviet Premier Khrushchev stated in a letter that missiles would be removed if the U.S. publicly guaranteed that it would not invade Cuba.

October 27 — News arrived that a U-2 had been shot down over Cuba and its pilot killed.

October 28 — The crisis ended. Khrushchev announced on Radio Moscow that Soviet missiles in Cuba were being dismantled.

The very next day, the U.S. agreed to comply with Indian Prime Minister Jawaharlal Nehru, who requested American military supplies to aid in its territorial battle with Red China. These busy — and trying — times wore on.

Francisco and an earlier one in New York meant 13 days were required to decide the outcome — tying a calendar record set during the rain-soaked 1911 Series. A packed house of almost 44,000 crammed Candlestick Park to witness what became an epic battle.

As a team, the Yankees batted a paltry .199 in the 1962 World Series. Roger Maris hit .174. Mickey Mantle slumped to a .120 mark. Their struggles continued in Game 7 against Stanford, who scattered seven hits in seven frames and gave up just one run. That came in the fifth, when Bill Skowron and Clete Boyer singled, Terry drew a walk and Tony Kubek grounded into a double play.

Stanford was sharp, but Terry was even better. He retired the first 17 Giants he faced, losing a no-hit bid to a Stanford single with two outs in the sixth inning. He had allowed just two hits entering the ninth, when pinch hitter Matty Alou led off by bunting for a single, bringing the home fans to their feet. Terry quieted them by striking out Felipe Alou and Chuck Hiller, bringing the Yankees to within an out of their 20th World Series title.

Willie Mays would not become that final out. The Giants slugger ripped a double to right field, and only a great defensive play by Maris held the potential tying run — in the form of Matty Alou — at third base. Logic held that Willie McCovey, a left-handed batter who had tripled in his previous trip to the plate, would be intentionally walked with first base open.

However, Houk shunned logic. While right-handed hitter Orlando Cepeda waited in the on-deck circle, Terry delivered a ball and a strike to McCovey. The next pitch was to Willie's liking, and he crushed it toward right field — a line drive that appeared destined to win a championship for San Francisco, and make Terry a two-time loser on the last swing of a World Series.

Many teams used to employ "gimmick" defensive alignments against McCovey in those days. They would put their second baseman in short right field or use their third baseman as a fourth outfielder, and then move the shortstop one way or the other to fill the gap. The Yankees were not among the teams that defended "Stretch" that way.

So after McCovey's line drive soared past Terry — with such velocity that not even a gale-force wind would have altered its path — second baseman Bobby Richardson was in position. He had just enough time to slide to his left and raise his glove. He snared the climbing ball in the webbing, making dramatic winners of Terry and the Yankees.

"He really was out of position," McCovey would say years later, referring to the "shifts" he normally faced. "If anybody should have caught it, it should have been the shortstop. Richardson would never admit that."

McCovey admitted that he used to dream about the play for years, and he was asked if the ball ever eluded Richardson's glove in those dreams. Did it ever find the right-field grass and trigger a Giants celebration? "Unfortunately," McCovey noted, "he keeps catching it."

The day after the Yankees celebrated in San Francisco and

Tom Tresh, New York Yankees left fielder, makes a spectacular grab of Giants center fielder Willie Mays' line drive in the seventh inning of Game 7 of the 1962 World Series on October 16, 1962. The play helped preserve the Yankees' thin 1-0 winning margin.

their fans spilled into the streets of New York for their seemingly annual autumn victory party, issues of far greater importance were coming to light. President Kennedy met with Soviet Foreign Minister Andrei Gromyko and advised him that America would not tolerate Soviet missiles in Cuba, amid denials of their existence.

Over the next 13 days, Americans sat on edge as the world's two superpowers teetered on the brink of nuclear war. By odd coincidence, the 1962 World Series had also lasted 13 days — but these were exuberant, thrilling days, when Americans had reveled in a classic baseball showdown between two major-league superpowers.

CHAPTER 15

CARDINALS FLY HIGH

1964 WORLD SERIES, GAME 7

Above: Clete Boyer, star Yankees infielder, may not have even been the best third baseman in his own family. His brother Ken was the 1964 National League MVP for the pennant-winning Cardinals. Both Boyers homered in the 1964 World Series, becoming the first siblings ever to do so in a fall classic. Bottom: Cardinals pitcher Bob Gibson is embraced by third baseman Ken Boyer, while catcher Tim McCarver rushes up to congratulate the right-hander. The celebration came after the final out in the seventh World Series game against the Yankees in St. Louis, on October 15, 1964, which the Cards won 7-5, with Gibson going all the way.

October 15, 1964 — St. Louis: Harry Caray made his way down from the radio broadcast booth to the box seats next to the Cardinals' dugout, where team owner August A. Busch, Jr., was sitting.

It was the ninth inning of the final game of the regular season, and with the Cardinals ahead of the Mets 11-5, what had been unthinkable a month earlier was now only moments away. It was hard to tell who was more excited, Caray or Busch.

Ed Kranepool stepped in to hit for the Mets against reliever Barney Schultz, and lofted a foul pop-up. Catcher Tim McCarver made the easy catch, and Caray began screaming into his microphone.

"The Cardinals win the pennant! The Cardinals win the pennant! The Cardinals win the pennant!"

Caray, and the rest of the Cardinals fans, could be excused for being excited. After all, it was the first time that the Cardinals had earned a berth in the World Series since 1946. In late August, with just over a month to play, they had trailed first-place Philadelphia by eleven games. Now, in the wake of the Phillies' collapse, the St. Louis Cardinals had a National League pennant — and an October 7 date with the New York Yankees for Game 1 of the 1964 World Series.

Since nobody had expected the Cardinals to win the pennant, it was understandable that they would be more relaxed than the Yankees. Still, seeing backup catcher Bob Uecker trying to catch fly balls with a tuba during batting practice before the first game broke any tension that might have existed — and behind a home run from St. Louis native Mike Shannon, the Cardinals won 9-5.

The Yankees regrouped to win Games 2 and 3, and after the Series moved to New York, jumped to a 3-0 lead in Game 4. The Yankees were now on the verge of taking a commanding, three games to one edge in the Series. The Cardinals loaded the bases in the sixth inning, however, and Ken Boyer connected

Opposite: St. Louis pitcher Bob Gibson seemed to be able to win games by sheer force of will, to say nothing of his incredible talent. Despite having very little left in the tank, he threw a complete-game 7-5 win to capture the deciding Game 7 of the 1964 World Series over the Yankees.

Cardinals catcher Tim McCarver scores on the front end of a double steal in the final game of the World Series at St. Louis on October 15, 1964. Yankees catcher Elston Howard could not handle a late throw by second baseman Bobby Richardson.

with an Al Downing pitch for a grand slam, putting St. Louis in front, 4-3.

Relief pitchers Roger Craig and Ron Taylor made the lead stand up for the final four innings, and the Series was tied at two wins each. Boyer, playing against his younger brother Clete, the third baseman for the Yankees, later called the grand slam the most important moment of his career.

"I can't remember anything in my career that had more impact," Boyer said. "I felt happiest because it brought us back even in the Series. If we had lost that game, we would have been down

LETTER OF RESIGNATION

On the day after the Cardinals won the 1964 World Series, manager Johnny Keane met with owner August A. Busch, Jr. The meeting was expected to be a formality, with Keane agreeing to a new contract.

Instead, Keane shocked Busch and the baseball world by handing in his letter of resignation. Angered by the firing of his good friend, the team's general manager Bing Devine, in August, Keane had decided to resign, even before he knew the Cardinals were going to win the National League pennant.

Keane's letter of resignation read:

Dear Mr. Busch:

This is to submit my resignation as field manager of the St. Louis Cardinals, effective at the end of the last championship National League game, whether it be the end of the regular season or at the completion of the World Series.

I want you to know that I have enjoyed working for you since you owned the Cardinals, as well as the many years I spent within the organization prior to that time.

I regret very much the necessity of this decision, especially severing the close relations I have had with so many of the Cardinals' personnel.

I wish also to express my gratitude to the City of St. Louis and to the St. Louis people for being so kind to me and my family for so many years, and to the Cardinals players who have been so loyal and to whom I am deeply indebted for a full effort 100 percent of the time.

I resign my position with the friendliest of feelings and wish nothing but success to you and your fine Cardinals team.

Four days later, Keane was hired as manager of the team the Cardinals had just defeated in the World Series — the New York Yankees.

three games to one. I can remember, as I ran around the bases, that the uppermost thought was that this might square the series. It did."

Bob Gibson started Game 5 for the Cardinals, and was just one out away from a 2-0 victory when Tom Tresh tied the game with a home run. The tie was short-lived, however, as McCarver delivered a three-run homer in the 10th that gave the Cardinals a 5-2 victory.

The Series shifted back to St. Louis, where the Yankees won Game 6 to tie the Series. The Yankees' victory meant that the 1964 World Series would go to seven games for the nineteenth time in World Series history. Gibson came back on two days rest to start for the Cardinals and the Yankees went with a rookie, Mel Stottlemyre, who had also started the fifth game.

Like the first six games in the Series, Game 7 began at one o'clock local time — two o'clock in New York — so those people watching television in New York could either tune into the ballgame or popular game shows like *Password* and *To Tell the Truth*. New Yorkers without access to a television or radio could get inning-by-inning updates by calling a special telephone recording set up by the New York Telephone Company.

On October 15th, as more than 30,000 fans jammed Sportsman's Park in St. Louis to watch Game 7, Hollywood released its latest blockbuster, the sweeping historical epic *The Fall of the Roman Empire*, starring Sophia Loren. As it turned out, Game 7 of the 1964 World Series would mark the beginning of the fall of the Yankees' baseball empire.

The Cardinals built a 6-0 lead before Mickey Mantle hit a three-run homer in the sixth inning;

it would turn out to be the eighteenth and final Series homer of Mantle's career. Ken Boyer homered in the seventh to extend the St. Louis lead to 7-3, and the score remained the same entering the ninth.

Solo homers by Phil Linz and Clete Boyer — the first and only time two brothers homered in the same World Series game — cut the lead to 7-5, but Cardinals' manager Johnny Keane stuck with an obviously tiring Gibson instead of going to the bullpen. The manager's faith was rewarded when Bobby Richardson popped out to second to end the game and the Series.

Gibson, who had played with the Harlem Globetrotters before beginning his baseball career, received a new Corvette sports car from *Sport Magazine* for being named the MVP of the Series. He set a Series record with 31 strikeouts in his three starts.

The Cardinals' clubhouse was chaotic, just as it had been in the pennant-winning celebration. Yet for some reason, Cardinals' manager Keane appeared somewhat removed from the raucous festivities — and the next day, the world found out why.

Hard-throwing right-hander Jim Bouton won two games in the 1964 World Series for the New York Yankees. His over-the-top style, however, led almost immediately to arm problems, and he was never the same pitcher after 1964.

A week earlier, before anybody knew what the rest of the season would bring, Keane had stayed up late one night, handwriting his letter of resignation to Busch, effective at the end of the season. Keane told nobody of his plans, however, as the Cardinals celebrated the team's first World Series title in eighteen years.

"How can you describe in words what we've done in 169 games?" asked McCarver as he stood in front of his locker. He then attempted to answer his own question. "You can't. This is the greatest bunch of players anywhere."

FOR LOVE

OF

THE GAME

CHAPTER 16

FDR: FRIEND OF THE GAME

PRESIDENTIAL BASEBALL

In his first eight years as United States president, Franklin D. Roosevelt attended 11 major-league baseball games — more than any other active chief executive before or since. And no president loved the game more. "Roosevelt enjoys himself at a ball game as much as a kid on Christmas morning," wrote Harold C. Burr in the June 1939 issue of *Baseball* magazine. "Once in the field box the present president believes again that there is a Santa Claus. He gets right into the spirit of the game, munches peanuts, applauds good plays and chuckles over bad ones."

As president, Roosevelt pulled America out of the Great Depression and led the nation nobly during World War II. He was reelected three times (serving from 1932 to 1945), both for his leadership skills and his zest for all things American.

Growing up in the 1880s and 1890s, Roosevelt often indulged in the national pastime. But, he lamented in his diary, "I do not play well." Not surprisingly, he was an adept field general, and in 1900 — the year his grandfather, Theodore Roosevelt, first ran for president — he served as

manager of the Groton prep school baseball team.

FDR was diagnosed with polio in 1921, yet the strong-willed politician won the governorship of New York in 1928 and the presidency four years later. From 1933 to 1938, he attended every Washington Senators Opening Day game, throwing out the first ball with an overhand lob and an exuberant grin. He told Senators owner Clark Griffith, "If I didn't have to hobble up those steps in front of all those people, I'd be out at the park every day."

Not much of a thrower, Roosevelt uncorked a wild one on Opening Day in 1940 that smashed the camera lens of *Washington Post* photographer Irving Schlossenberg. Roosevelt also threw out the first ball at two World Series and an All-Star Game. However, eight months after he attended the Senators' 1941 opener, his attention was greatly diverted: The Japanese attacked Pearl Harbor.

Even during global warfare, Roosevelt remained a friend of the game. On January 15, 1942, he sent his famous "green light" letter to Major League Baseball Commissioner Kenesaw Mountain Landis. Roosevelt wrote: "I honestly feel that it would be best for the country to keep baseball going. There will be fewer people unemployed and everybody will work longer hours and harder than ever before. And that means that they ought to have a chance for recreation and for taking their minds off their work even more than before."

Roosevelt made two requests from the commissioner, both of which would be granted: that able-bodied big-leaguers serve in the Armed Forces during the war. And that more night games be scheduled so that citizens who worked hard during the day could enjoy ball games in the evening.

FDR, however, would never see another major-league game. He died on April 12, 1945 —12 years to the day after attending his first game as United States president.

President Franklin D. Roosevelt puts his all into baseball's official no. 1 heave of 1938, preceding the season-opening Senators-Athletics battle in Washington, April 18, 1938. Others are, left to right, Athletics manager Connie Mack; Senators owner Clark Griffith; and Bucky Harris, Senators manager.

Opposite: The Presidential wing of the U.S. Government inaugurated the 1936 baseball campaign on April 14 in Washington. President Franklin D. Roosevelt tosses out the season's first pitch. Yankees manager Joe McCarthy and Senators skipper Bucky Harris are at the president's right.

CHAPTER 17

HECK OF A VEECK

THERE FOR "THE LITTLE GUY"

Bill Veeck's plaque in the National Baseball Hall of Fame ends with the line: "A Champion of the Little Guy." That was never more true than on August 19, 1951, when the St. Louis Browns owner sent a 43-inch, 65-pound batter to the plate to draw a four-pitch walk in a game against the Detroit Tigers. However, being there for "the little guy" went far beyond the memorable Eddie Gaedel stunt for Veeck, the son of a sportswriter who later became Chicago Cubs president.

money's worth at the park; and he spent his entire career trying to ensure that each one did. He usually succeeded.

There were many reasons not to go to the ballpark in the mid-1950s, and major-league attendance in many cities reflected it. The New York teams — particularly the Yankees and Dodgers — dominated their respective leagues, leaving fans in many other cities out in the proverbial cold. Television also brought major-league games into the

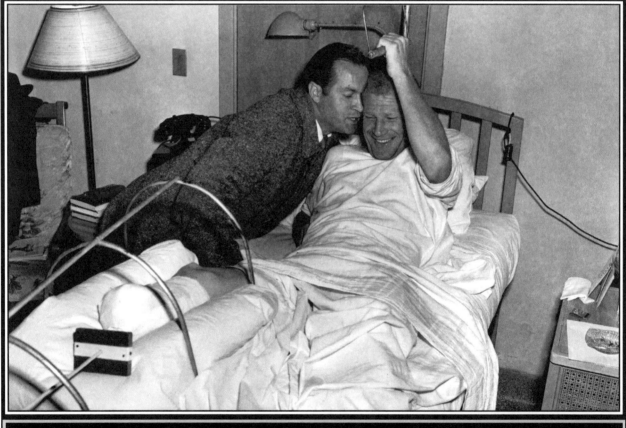

Bob Hope, part owner of the Cleveland Indians, visits Indians president Bill Veeck at Cleveland Clinic in Ohio, Nov. 7, 1946. Veeck is recovering from amputation of his right leg, injured at Bougainville, France while he was in the Marines during World War II.

From his days as an 11-year-old selling soda, mailing out tickets and planting ivy on the walls at Wrigley Field, to his many years as owner of the Indians, Browns and White Sox, Veeck cared first and foremost for the little guy — the fan who turned over hard-earned dollars for a ticket to the game. Veeck felt that every fan should get his or her

fans' living rooms for free. Many fans therefore chose to watch their cities' struggling ballclubs on television, rather than in person.

Just five years after winning a pennant, the 1952 Boston Braves drew less than 3,700 fans per home game. Two years later, the Philadelphia Athletics averaged fewer than 4,000 themselves. It marked the third time in five years that the once-proud A's had attracted less than 5,000 per home date. And the St. Louis Browns had it worse than any of them. Between 1949 and 1953, they only drew more than 4,000 fans to a home game just one time. Suffice it to say, the turnstiles outside New York City were not exactly spinning with baseball fans.

If anyone proved capable of changing that, it was Veeck, who at age 27 purchased the near-bankrupt American Association club in Milwaukee in 1941. There, he tried spur-of-the-moment promotions, giving away everything from live animals to beer. He cleaned up the ballpark, hired bands to entertain, scheduled 8:30 a.m. games to accommodate shift workers and set minor-league attendance records. He wound up selling the club for a considerable profit before serving a Marine tour in World War II.

Though injured in combat, Veeck came home determined to make his mark in baseball. He led a

Series since 1920.

While many team owners sat with their wealthy friends and kept clear of the masses, Veeck provided a refreshing change of pace. He never wore a tie, which in itself set him apart. And he spent a considerable amount of time sitting in the stands, not only talking with the fans, but listening to them. It was there that he picked up his best ideas about how to make a trip to a ball game an enjoyable experience for everyone, from giving away door prizes to stitching players' names on their uniforms so fans could identify them more easily.

Of course, Veeck's stunts went further than any fan would dare suggest. Gaedel's appearance was a shining example of that. The Browns were some 50 games out of first place during that 1951 season, the year Veeck purchased the club. He hired the three feet, seven inch tall Gaedel to pop out of a cake between games of a doubleheader. Veeck then sent

Eddie Gaedel, all three-feet, seven-inches of him, makes his first and only big-league plate appearance on August 19, 1951, at St. Louis' Sportsman's Park. Gaedel, signed as a publicity stunt by St. Louis Browns owner Bill Veeck, drew a four-pitch walk from Detroit hurler Bob Cain. Two days later, AL president Will Harridge banned Gaedel from the game.

syndicate that bought the Indians in 1946 and doubled their attendance to 1.5 million the following year. The 1947 campaign saw him sign Larry Doby from the Negro Leagues, breaking the American League color line. The next year he added legendary black pitcher Satchel Paige — the oldest rookie in history — and the Indians won their first World

him to the plate as a pinch hitter — wearing the number 1/8 on his back — in the first inning of the second game. The Tigers protested, but the Browns produced a contract approved by the league office, and Gaedel took his stance. It was a crouch that left Detroit pitcher Bob Cain with a strike zone the size of a shoebox. Four high pitches later, Gaedel had the free pass Veeck had hoped for, and the very next day American League president Will Harridge banned "little people" from the game.

Undaunted, Veeck staged what might have been an even better promotion five days later. Sportsman's Park fans were invited to "manage" a game against the A's using "yes" and "no" placards. Before making any decisions, Browns skipper Zack Taylor was to consult with the crowd by holding up signs with questions like, "Shall we warm up a new pitcher?" Majority vote ruled, and St. Louis snapped a four-game losing streak with a 5-3 win.

Always maintaining that fans were the heart and soul of the game, Veeck later bolstered interest in the White Sox with baseball's first exploding scoreboard and several more memorable promotions. Of his legacy, Veeck once wrote: "No one has to tell me that if I returned to baseball tomorrow, won ten

Leroy "Satchel" Paige, 46 years old, signs his 1953 contract with the St. Louis Browns as owner Bill Veeck looks on. Amidst all the stunts and fan-pleasing innovations instituted by Veeck, it is forgotten that he was also an early civil rights pioneer, signing Larry Doby as the AL's first black player and bringing Paige, a Negro Leagues legend, to the majors.

straight pennants and left all the old attendance records moldering in the dust, I would still be remembered, in the end, as the man who sent a midget up to bat ... I have always found humor in the incongruous, I have always tried to entertain."

Veeck won a second AL pennant as owner of Chicago's 1959 "Go-Go" Sox, but in the end, he was right. Despite the attendance records he set and the titles his teams earned, it was the zany stunt, the wacky promotion and the dedication to making the game of baseball fun for which he would be remembered. Veeck himself could not have schemed up a more fitting tribute.

VEECK'S GREATEST GIMMICKS

Baseball, first and foremost, is a game. And even with his vast business sense, Bill Veeck understood that perhaps better than anyone. Below is a sampling of the fun this man brought to the game during his career. Veeck:

- Helped plant, as a youth, the ivy on the walls of Wrigley Field.
- Ordered more comfortable seats, cleaner restrooms and better concessions at ballparks to improve the fan experience.
- Once gave his manager a needed left-handed arm by having the new pitcher jump out of a cake.
- Greeted patrons as they entered the park or while in their seats, sharing a beverage while listening to their recommendations.
- Scheduled games as early as 8:30 a.m. so shift workers could attend.
- Integrated the American League, signing Larry Doby to be its first black player in 1947. The next year, he added 42-year-old Satchel Paige, the oldest "rookie" in history, to the Indians' roster and won a World Series.
- Held a ceremonial burial of Cleveland's 1948 flag when it became apparent the Indians would not defend their pennant in 1949.
- Sent three-feet seven-inch tall Eddie Gaedel to the plate for the Browns in a 1951 game to draw a four-pitch walk against the Tigers — perhaps baseball's best-known publicity stunt.
- Allowed Browns fans to make managerial decisions by majority vote, using large placards that directed skipper Zack Taylor when to call for a bunt, steal or pitching change. The team ended a four-game losing streak.
- Installed Major League Baseball's first exploding scoreboard at Comiskey Park, a 130-foot monster that launched fireworks, produced sound effects and set off electric pinwheels every time a White Sox player hit a home run.

CHAPTER 18

THE GAME IKE LIKED

EISENHOWER EMBRACES THE NATIONAL PASTIME

Dwight Eisenhower once recalled a conversation he had as a boy in his home state of Kansas: "[A] friend of mine and I went fishing, and as we sat there in the warmth of the summer afternoon on a riverbank, we talked about what we wanted to do when we grew up. I told him that I wanted to be a real major-league baseball player, a genuine professional like Honus Wagner. My friend said that he'd like to be president of the United States. Neither of us got our wish."

Eisenhower worked hard to pursue his baseball dream, but he was no Honus Wagner — the legendary shortstop of the Pittsburgh Pirates. "Ike" played center field in a semipro league after high school, and he made the junior varsity team at West Point. But he didn't make West Point's varsity squad, which he called "one of the greatest disappointments of my life, maybe my greatest."

Ironically, Eisenhower would find the battlefield easier than the ballfield. As a general during World War II, he commanded the D-Day forces that stormed the beaches of Normandy and eventually liberated Europe from Nazi tyranny. Idolized across America for his leadership, strength of character, and upstanding values, Eisenhower was elected president in 1952 (under the slogan "I Like Ike"), and then reelected in 1956. In his eight years as commander-in-chief, Eisenhower — well familiar with the horrors of war — skillfully kept the United States at peace. As such, he occasionally could indulge in his favorite pastime: baseball.

In seven of his eight years as president, Eisenhower threw out the first ball on Opening Day at Griffith Stadium, home of the American League's Washington Senators. While in office, he attended 13 big-league contests, including Game 1 of the 1956 World Series at Yankee Stadium. Ike didn't witness Don Larsen's perfect game in Game 5, but he congratulated the Yankee hero with a personal letter: "It has been so long since anyone pitched a perfect big-league game that I have to go back to my generation of ballplayers to recall such a thing — and that is truly a long time ago. This note brings you my very sincere congratulations on a memorable feat, one that will inspire pitchers for a long time to come."

Eisenhower clearly held the game close to his heart. In 1954 he presented the Senators' Mickey Vernon with his batting championship trophy. And in 1957, Eisenhower invited Mexico's Little League world champions to the White House. On February 17, 1954, during a particularly quiet month, Ike set aside time to write to his boyhood hero, Honus Wagner, who was about to celebrate his 80th birthday. In a letter that he labeled "personal and confidential," Eisenhower wrote: "Realization that you now count your years at the four score mark reminds me, with something of a shock, that it was fifty years ago that I used to follow your batting average with the keenest of interest."

For Eisenhower, who had conquered the global enemy and become leader of the free world, baseball was his "Rosebud": a sweet reminder of childhood that he treasured till his dying days.

Eisenhower, who played center field in a semipro league after high school, chats with one of the greatest ever at the position: the Yankees' Mickey Mantle.

THE BABE

CHAPTER 19

RUTH'S CALLED SHOT

1932 WORLD SERIES, GAME 3

October 1, 1932 — Chicago: After the "Black Sox Scandal" of 1919, Babe Ruth had almost single-handedly resuscitated baseball's popularity through a winning combination of charisma and the long ball, which he brought into play.

By 1932, however, the fans' excitement for the aging slugger had waned as Ruth's girth had increased and his game slowed. But Ruth pulled his game together and showed everyone that the tank wasn't empty just yet by leading the Yankees to the 1932 World Series, when he hit .341, with 41 home runs and 137 RBI.

The 1932 World Series would take place against the grim backdrop of America in the throes of the Great Depression. As 1932 drew to a close, over 11 million Americans remained out of work. For the first time in the nation's history, more people were actually leaving the United States than coming into the country. Promising a "New Deal" for the country, Franklin Delano Roosevelt accepted the Democratic presidential nomination.

Meanwhile, the Yankees prepared to square off in the World Series against the Chicago Cubs. To say that there was no love lost between these teams would have been a gross understatement; in fact, some very bad blood existed between the Yankees and Cubs.

For starters, Yankees manager Joe McCarthy had been given the boot by Chicago in 1930 — a year after he'd guided them to a NL pennant.

As for Ruth, he especially hated the Cubs for their cavalier treatment of his friend, former Yankee Mark Koenig. Although Koenig had played a huge role in guiding the Cubs to a NL pennant, the team had only voted him half a World Series share. Ruth was so rankled by Chicago's slight of his old friend that he browbeat the Cubs throughout the Series. During batting practice prior to Game 3, Ruth shouted to the "damn bum Cubs" that they wouldn't be making a return trip to Yankee Stadium. Since the Yankees had won the first two games in New York, Ruth was effectively telling the Cubs the Yankees planned to wrap up the Series in Chicago.

Batting practice only added to the Yankees' mystique. Ruth's first swing in batting practice produced a tumultuous blast that almost went out of Wrigley Field. He continued the display in front of the awestruck Cubs fans and Lou Gehrig followed suit. The powerful display gave the Yankees a psychological advantage. After all, what mortal could possibly stop such baseball immortals?

By game time, a crowd of 49,986 packed the stands waiting for the start of Game 3. Charlie Root

Artist Robert Thom's depiction of Babe Ruth's "called shot" in Game 3 of the 1932 World Series at Chicago's Wrigley Field on October 1, 1932. Ruth's fifth-inning homer, his second of the game, put the Yankees up 5-4 (Courtesy Baseball Hall of Fame and Museum).

started for the Cubs and immediately got into trouble, when Earle Combs led off the first for the Yankees and hit the ball to Billy Jurges. The Cubs shortstop was playing in place of the injured Koenig and promptly threw the ball into the Yankees' dugout.

Instead of having one out heading into the meat of the Yankees' order, Root now had a man on second. The mistake appeared to fluster Root and the right-hander walked the next batter, Joey Sewell, to bring up Ruth.

The memory of Ruth's batting practice display had to be circulating through the minds of every Cubs fan in Wrigley — particularly Root's. The Cubs pitcher threw two balls wide before delivering a pitch

Here's where accounts of the game began to vary.

In Ruth's third at-bat, was he thinking about teaching the crowd a lesson, taunting the Cubs, or both, when he delivered his memorable theatrics?

Root got strike one on Ruth, who watched the pitch pass and then raised his finger for the first strike. He did the same thing when Root delivered his second strike against two balls.

Ruth then stepped out of the batter's box and pointed. But where was the 38-year-old Yankee pointing? Was he pointing at Root, the Cubs' bench, or was he forecasting that the next pitch would be deposited over the wall in center field?

Root delivered and Ruth took a mighty pass at

Seven of the Chicago Cubs' eight pitchers gather prior to the 1932 World Series. From left are Bob Smith, Charley Root, Guy Bush, Bud Tinning, Jake May, Pat Malone, and Lon Warneke. The eighth Cubs hurler, Burleigh Grimes — the last man allowed to throw spitballs legally in the majors — is not pictured.

that Ruth found to his liking. He swung and connected, sending a blast over the stands in right field to put the Yankees up 3-0.

When Ruth ran out to the outfield to play defense, he was greeted with playful boos and lemons, which rained from the stands. Typical of Ruth's style, he tipped his cap and smiled at the crowd. They continued to taunt him until Ruth stepped into the batter's box in the fifth inning with the score tied at 4-4. Greeting him was a lone lemon that rolled to the plate.

the ball, sending an arcing shot that seemed to linger in the air as it covered more and more distance. Center fielder Johnny Moore gave chase to the ball, but then simply stopped and watched its trajectory. The ball split the middle of the field before ducking out of sight at the base of the flagpole at a corner where the scoreboard and the end of the right-field bleachers met — an estimated 436 feet from home plate.

The blast provided the longest ball ever hit at Wrigley Field to that point in time and gave Ruth his

15th career World Series home run.

Ruth continued to jaw while enthusiastically rounding the bases. Instead of boos, Cubs fans now hailed him with raucous cheers. Ruth issued a curse to each Cub infielder when he passed by and when he reached third base he took a moment to bow to the Cubs' bench.

Calling his shot added additional fodder to Ruth's supreme legend. Lost in the Ruth hype was the fact Gehrig also hit two home runs in the game. As for the Cubs, they made a valiant effort to come back before losing, 7-5. The Yankees then wrapped up the Series in Game 4, crushing the Cubs 13-6, to complete the sweep.

Chicago Cubs right-hander Charley Root, who won 15 games in 1932, but is best remembered for delivering the pitch in the fifth inning of that year's World Series Game 3 that Babe Ruth slammed for a home run after supposedly "calling his shot."

Days later, *Chicago Tribune* columnist Westbrook Pegler wrote of Ruth's display noting "the people who saw Babe Ruth play that ball game and hit those two home runs against the Cubs came away from the baseball plant with a spiritual memento of the most gorgeous display of humor, athletic art and championship class any performer in any game has ever presented."

In an October 2003 *Baseball Digest* article, former Yankees Charlie Devens, who was at the game that day, said Ruth never denied that he was pointing to the stands. But even though he doubted that Ruth was indeed calling his shot, Devens added, "Still, it was quite extraordinary to see him point, then hit the very next pitch out of the ballpark."

BABE'S FALL CLASSICS

Babe Ruth, idol of millions due to his swaggering style, fun-loving grin, and matchless production at the plate.

Babe Ruth and great feats in the World Series walk hand in hand into baseball history. Ruth is one of two players in baseball history to hit three home runs in one World Series game — and he turned the trick twice. In 1926 the Yankees played the Cardinals in the World Series when Ruth hit three home runs at Sportsman's Park in St. Louis. Despite Ruth's Game 4 heroics, the Cardinals won the Series in seven games.

In 1928 the Yankees again played the Cardinals in the World Series, but this time, the Yankees won in a sweep. Ruth connected for three home runs in Game 4 and finished with a .625 batting average for the World Series. Reggie Jackson is the only other player to ever hit three home runs in one World Series game.

Equally impressive is the pitching record Ruth holds by pitching the longest complete game in World Series history. In 1916, when he pitched for the Red Sox, Ruth won a 2-1, 14-inning decision over the Brooklyn Dodgers.

CHAPTER 20

UNCLE BABE

A CHRISTMAS WISH

In 1947 Babe Ruth could no longer deliver joy to fans with his majestic home runs. In fact, he could barely walk . . . or even talk. The Babe was dying of cancer. Yet one thing he still could do was make children happy. That December, Ruth painfully pulled on a Santa Claus suit, beard and all, and handed presents to young victims of polio at the Hotel Astor in New York. Their faces illuminated the room.

All his adult life, Ruth maintained a special fondness for young people. Some believe he felt comfortable around kids because he himself had never grown up. More likely, he simply enjoyed making them smile whenever he rubbed their heads or handed them an autograph.

After ball games and at special appearances, Ruth spent up to several hours signing autographs. He couldn't bear the thought of any tyke going home disappointed. In New York and on the road, the Babe frequently visited hospitalized children. In 1931 alone, he played Santa Claus for hundreds of kids at city hospitals. He also felt compelled to visit orphanages — undoubtedly because of his experience at Saint Mary's Industrial School for Boys. Because his parents were unable to care for him, the Babe spent most of his childhood at the boarding school.

According to legend, Ruth even hit home runs for a dying boy. During the 1926 World Series against the Cardinals, the Babe had heard that one

Youngsters lend an ear to Babe Ruth as he tells them stories of his life from orphanage to baseball fame, November 29, 1924. Ruth loved kids and gave them a lot of his time.

of his fans, young Johnny Sylvester, lay on his deathbed after falling from a horse. Ruth supposedly sent Johnny a telegram, promising that he would hit a home run for him in that day's contest (Game 4). He responded with a homer in the first inning . . . and another in the third . . . and one more in the sixth.

In reality, the Yankees had sent Johnny an autographed baseball, but no one had promised him a home run. Nevertheless, after Johnny got out of the hospital (he wasn't dying after all), Ruth drove to his house and chatted with the boy. Johnny was one of thousands of children who forever cherished their moments with baseball's biggest hero.

As the weather turned cold in 1947, Ruth realized (correctly) that he might have just one Christmas left on earth. As sick as he was, he displayed kindness and patience with children as they sat on his lap and told him the presents they wanted. One little girl asked for a baby brother. "Oh, now a baby brother," Ruth said, contemplating. "We'll wait awhile, a little while, about that, and then I'll let you know more about it."

Afterward, the Babe pulled down his beard and addressed the cameras and microphones. Through a terribly throaty voice, he spoke with the utmost sincerity: "I want to take this opportunity," he said, "to wish all the children — not only in America, but all over the world — a very merry Christmas."

CHAPTER 21

SO LONG, BABE

THE BAMBINO PASSES ON

Top: Four days after this photo was taken (May 21, 1935), Ruth belted three home runs in one game — including a blast clear out of Forbes Field. He would never homer again. Bottom: James Keane, a retired New York City patrolman, lifts his seven-year-old son to see Ruth's body. Many youngsters wore their Little League uniforms to the viewing at Yankee Stadium.

An overweight Babe Ruth, looking older than his 40 years in his Boston Braves uniform, stepped into the batter's box at Pittsburgh's Forbes Field on May 25, 1935. The Bambino had already homered twice in the game, and now in the seventh, he dug in against the Pirates' Guy Bush. Unloading on a curveball, Ruth rocketed a tremendous blast to right field — 50 feet over the double-deck roof — making it the first ball ever hit out of Forbes Field in its 26-year history.

"Boy," bellowed Babe as he took a seat on the bench, "that last one felt good."

A light bulb often shines brightest before it burns out, and such was the case with Babe Ruth. He had endured a miserable spring in 1935, his first year with the Braves: bad knees and ankles, a nagging cold, and a batting average in the .100s. His moon shot at Forbes was the last of his 714 career home runs. After injuring his knee on May 30, he never played another big-league game.

Ruth had known he was at the end of the line when he signed with the Braves, but he had hoped the new gig would lead to a managerial position with the team. He had asked other teams about managing, including the Yankees and Tigers, but was denied every time. Ruth thought that the woeful Braves (who would finish 38-115 in 1935) might give him a shot, but owner Judge Emil Fuchs wouldn't oblige.

Since the late teens, Ruth had ruled baseball like an emperor, thanks to his exuberance, charm, and legendary skill. Yet to owners he was an irresponsible kid who never grew up — unfit as a ballclub leader. The Babe was too naive to realize his shortcomings. He kept praying for a managerial offer, but it never came. "It was the biggest disappointment of his life," said his daughter, Julia Ruth Stevens, "no question about it."

Frustrated and sometimes depressed to be out of the spotlight, Ruth had enough diversions to keep him busy. He excelled at hunting (with his keen eye), golf (booming drives), and bowling. He enjoyed *The Lone Ranger* on radio as well as quiet evenings with his wife Claire and daughter Julia.

Opposite: On June 13, 1948, 25 years to the day after christening Yankee Stadium with a home run, Babe used a bat as a crutch during the ceremony at which his former team permanently retired #3 from the Yankee roster.

The Cleveland Indians display their adoration for the Bambino on June 13, 1948. Undoubtedly, many of them grew up dreaming of becoming the next Babe Ruth.

Of course, he still drew huge crowds of admirers wherever he went. In June 1938, Brooklyn Dodgers executive Larry MacPhail noticed the throngs of fans begging Babe for an autograph and realized he'd be a great gate attraction as a first base coach. Babe accepted, thinking again that it might lead to a managing job. That was another pipe dream (especially after he brawled with team captain Leo Durocher), but Babe enjoyed being at the ballpark anyway. He spent at least an hour after every game signing autographs, scrawling away until every young fan went home happy. He also gave 13-year-old clubhouse boy Donald Davidson a story to tell when he asked, "Hey kid, you like to play catch?"

Ruth's longtime teammate, Lou Gehrig, died on June 2, 1941. Hired to play himself in *The Pride of the Yankees*, the Hollywood film about Gehrig, Ruth shed 45 pounds to look like his old self. During World War II, Babe worked hard to raise funds for his country. He played a golf exhibition against Ty Cobb and batted against pitching great Walter Johnson. In appearances and on the radio, he urged Americans to contribute to the cause. He bought $100,000 worth of war bonds, and he visited four or five military hospitals a week. A decade after retirement, he was still the most popular athlete in America, hands down.

In 1945 MacPhail and others purchased the Yankees, and Ruth got excited again. He informed MacPhail that he'd like to manage the team, or at least the farm club in Newark. Weeks later, MacPhail wrote back, stating that both positions were already

RUTHIAN FEATS

On July 12, 1921, Babe Ruth belted his 137th career home run to break Roger Connor's major-league record. By the time of his retirement in 1935, the Babe had more than quintupled Connor's total, finishing with 714 circuit clouts. Although Hank Aaron surpassed that record in 1974, other feats remain solely Ruthian. Here is but a sampling:

• After being sold by the Boston Red Sox to the New York Yankees prior to the 1920 season, Ruth out-homered the entire Boston team in 10 of the next 12 campaigns.

• In the American League in 1920, 14.6 percent of all home runs — 54 of 369 — were hit by the Babe. Today, a slugger would have to crack close to 400 homers in a season to achieve 14.6 percent of the league total.

• Ruth eclipsed 40 home runs 11 times from 1920 through 1932, with highs of 60, 59, and 54 (twice).

• Babe led the American League in longballs 12 times.

• Ruth's career .690 slugging percentage (total bases divided by at-bats) remains the highest ever. He led the AL in slugging 13 times.

• Babe batted over .370 six times, with a high of .393 in 1923. His .342 batting average is the 10th best in major-league history.

• Ruth's career record as a pitcher was 94-46 with a 2.28 ERA. He is universally regarded as the greatest hitting pitcher, the best pitching hitter, and the greatest player, period, in baseball history.

filled. "Babe walked into the kitchen, numb," Claire later wrote. "It was the same kitchen where he had sat before on a chair, head in hands, and wept in fury and frustration. He wept once again."

Around the same time, Ruth experienced a severe pain over his left eye. By November, the left side of his face was swollen and he couldn't eat solid foods. He checked into a hospital, where he remained for a month before doctors determined the source of his malady: A malignant tumor had grown in the left side of his neck.

Babe had surgery on January 5, 1947, but doctors could not remove all of the cancer. He remained in the hospital, in pain and depressed, for another six weeks, losing approximately 100 pounds. Thousands of get-well letters poured in, and when he was finally released on February 15, hundreds of fans greeted him outside the hospital. He cried again.

Fearing that the Bambino wasn't long for the world, baseball commissioner Happy Chandler declared April 27 "Babe Ruth Day." Ruth arrived at Yankee Stadium in a camel's hair overcoat. Gray-haired and shaky, the Babe nonetheless delivered a heartfelt address to an enraptured crowd of 58,000. "The only real game in the world, I think, is baseball," he said in a raspy voice. "You've got to let it grow up with you, and if you're successful and you try hard enough, you're bound to come out on top, just like these boys have come to the top now."

Thanks to a regimen of experimental drugs, Ruth's health improved in the summer of 1947, but he fell into decline over the winter. On June 13, 1948, he appeared in Yankee Stadium in honor of the 25th anniversary of the ballpark. His Yankees pinstripes fit like baggy pajamas, and he used his bat as a crutch. On August 15, 1948, the Babe died in a hospital bed, shortly after signing his autobiography for one of his nurses. He was just 53 years old.

As Ruth's body lay in state at Yankee Stadium, with the flag at half-mast, more than 100,000 mourners filed past his casket. Little Leaguers came in uniform, and vendors sold hot dogs — the Babe's favorite snack. At his funeral, 75,000 swarmed New York's St. Patrick's Cathedral. Former Yankees Joe Dugan and Waite Hoyt were among those who served as pallbearers. It was a hot, sticky day, and as they left the cathedral Dugan whispered to Hoyt, "Lord, I'd give my right arm for an ice-cold beer right now."

Hoyt replied, "So would the Babe."

Ruth leaves hospital with male nurse Frank Delaney for a plane trip to Baltimore where he is to appear at a charity game on July 3, 1948. He would return to the hospital after the event and would then pass away there on August 15, the same year.

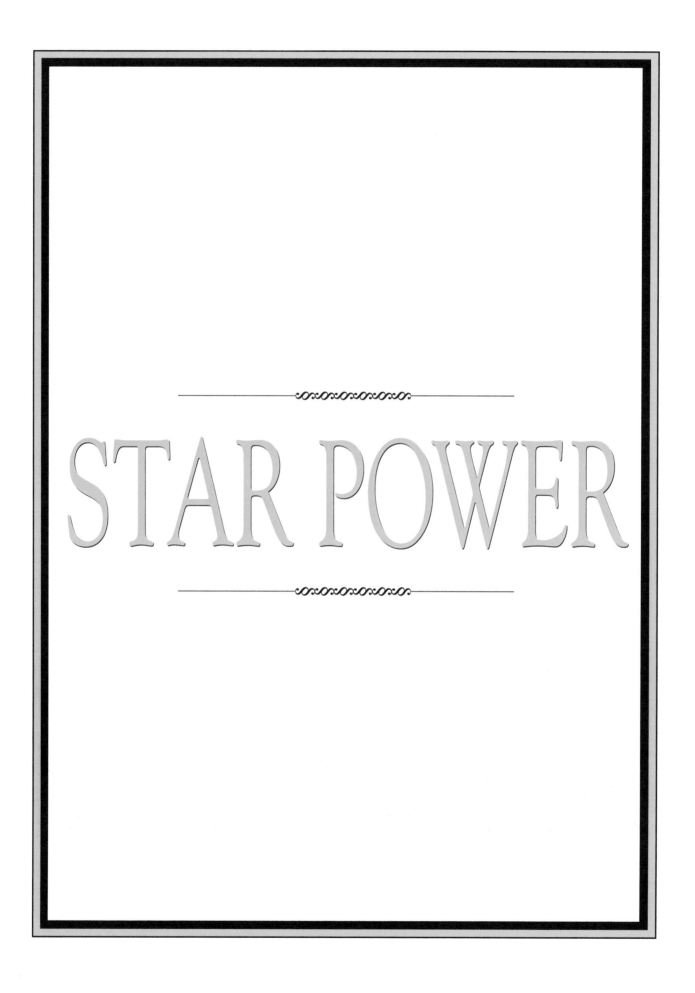

STAR POWER

CHAPTER 22

STAR BURST

1933 ALL-STAR GAME

July 6, 1933 — Chicago: Comiskey Park sounded like some far away paradise where Babe Ruth, Lou Gehrig, Frankie Frisch and other baseball greats would gather to do battle like immortals at Mount Olympus.

Or so went the breathless hype surrounding Major League Baseball's first All-Star Game, billed as "The Game of the Century." The United States was in the midst of the Great Depression and baseball was a national obsession. The very idea of a collection of National League stars playing a group from the American League stoked the imagination of any baseball fan with a pulse.

Like most cities in the United States, Chicago was feeling the sting of the Depression in 1933, when the city of "broad shoulders" celebrated its centennial. Ed Kelly reigned as the mayor of Chicago and called Bertie McCormick, the *Chicago Tribune* publisher, to see if the newspaper could help arrange a major sporting event during the city's "Century of Progress" exhibition at the World's Fair. McCormick immediately contacted the *Tribune*'s sports editor

The American League team poses before the first major-league All-Star Game in Chicago, July 6, 1933. The American League won 4-2. Front row, from left: Al Schacht, Eddie Collins, Tony Lazzeri, General Crowder, Jimmie Foxx, Art Fletcher, Earl Averill, Ed Rommel, Ben Chapman, Rick Ferrell, Sam West, Charlie Gehringer, batboy. Back row, from left: batboy, unidentified team member, Lou Gehrig, Babe Ruth, Oral Hildebrand, Connie Mack, Joe Cronin, Lefty Grove, batboy, Bill Dickey, Al Simmons, Lefty Gomez, Wes Ferrell, Jimmy Dykes, clubhouse boy.

Arch Ward, a crackerjack writer and born promoter.

In no time, Ward came up with the idea of staging an exhibition game between players from the American and National Leagues. A schmoozer par excellence, Ward told baseball moguls that the exhibition would be an asset for the game. But there were problems, like dealing with the major league schedule and getting players to the game. And there was always the possibility that a player might get injured while playing in a meaningless game. These concerns were enough to make the chances of holding an All-Star Game appear remote. Ward persisted, however, and on May 18, 1933, the 16 major-league club owners agreed to have the game played for one year. The *Tribune* agreed to underwrite the expenses for the game and the profits would be given to the Association of Professional Baseball Players of America, baseball's charity organization.

Ward took it upon himself to select the managers for the game: Connie Mack of the Philadelphia Athletics for the American League and John McGraw, formerly of the New York Giants, for the National League. Mack and McGraw had last

newspapers nationwide and those totals were sent to the *Tribune* to be tallied.

On July 6, 1933, a capacity crowd of 49,200 crowded into Comiskey Park to see which of the two leagues could claim bragging rights for being the superior league.

Mack sent Yankees left-hander Vernon "Lefty" Gomez to the mound to start for the American Leaguers. Despite having pitched on July 4, he held the senior circuit scoreless for the first three innings.

Meanwhile, McGraw sent Willie Hallahan to the hill to start for the National League. Like Gomez, the St. Louis left-hander was pitching on one day's rest after a start in which he'd pitched nine innings; Hallahan, however, did not prove to be as resilient as Grove. Of course, the fact that he was facing such AL icons as Babe Ruth, Lou Gehrig and Jimmy Simmons

The National League team, prior to the first major-league All-Star Game. Front row, from left: batboy Hasbrook, Pepper Martin, Lon Warneke, Tony Cuccinello. Middle row, from left: Bill Hallahan, Dick Bartell, Bill Terry, Bill McKechnie, John McGraw, Max Carey, Chick Hafey, Chuck Klein, Lefty O'Doul, Wally Berger. Back row, from left: Gabby Hartnett, Hack Wilson, Frankie Frisch, Carl Hubbell, Bill Walker, Paul Waner, Woody English, Hal Schumacher, Pie Traynor, trainer Andy Lotshaw.

managed against each other in the 1913 World Series, when the A's had defeated the Giants, four games to one.

Selecting the players became a matter for baseball fans throughout the country. Fans were given the chance to vote via a public ballot held by

probably didn't speed Hallahan's recovery time.

Hallahan got through the first inning before encountering his first smattering of trouble in the second. Ironically, it wasn't Ruth, Gehrig or even Simmons who delivered against Hallahan to get the American League going — it was Groves. After

Hallahan walked Dykes and Joe Cronin, Gomez stepped to the plate. Known far and wide as one of the worst hitters in the game, Gomez delivered a single to center field, driving home the first run in All-Star Game history for a 1-0 American League lead. Nor did it bode well for Hallahan in the third, when Charlie Gehringer walked, bringing Ruth to the plate.

With his broad belly and chubby cheeks, Ruth no longer resembled the athlete he'd been in his prime. But he remained the game's most popular figure by a landslide, carrying with him a regal status in the eyes of players and fans alike. Prior to the game, Ruth drew autograph-seeking fans toward him like the Pied Piper of the national pastime.

The crowd roared when Ruth moved into the

St. Louis Cardinal Pitcher William Hallahan warms up.

batter's box. Only the year before he had made his presence known in Chicago when he dismantled the Cubs in the 1932 World Series. Now Ruth was again gracing the Windy City with his presence. And he gave the fans what they wanted to see.

Hallahan tried to slip a fastball past the left-handed hitting Ruth and the "Sultan of Swat" connected, sending a line drive down the right field line that curled around the right field foul pole to give the American League a 3-0 lead.

The final score: American League 4, National League 2.

Receipts of the inaugural All-Star Game totaled $51,000, a huge sum in Depression-era America. Thus began one of the most popular and enduring events in Major League Baseball, thereafter known as the midsummer classic.

LITTLE NAPOLEON

The legendary John McGraw (left), manager of the first NL All-Star team, shakes hands with Boston Braves manager Bill McKechnie in 1930. McKechnie served as one of McGraw's coaches in the 1933 All-Star Game.

John McGraw was retired when he returned to baseball on July 6, 1933 to manage the National League in the first All-Star Game in major-league history. His participation was the final chapter for one of the more storied figures in baseball history.

As a player, McGraw was known as a feisty third baseman for the Baltimore Orioles in the 1890s before the major leagues were created. During his playing days he was credited with helping to develop the hit-and-run, the Baltimore chop, the squeeze play and other strategic moves. McGraw would do anything to win and was well known for detering baserunners by tripping or blocking them while a lone umpire watched the ball. Some have speculated that McGraw's tactics eventually led to the addition of umpires on the basepaths.

Despite McGraw's success as a player — he hit .334 in 16 seasons — the man who came to be known as "Little Napoleon" is best remembered for his managing skills. McGraw managed the New York Giants for 31 years and his team won 10 pennants, finished second 11 times and won three World Series. He ranks second all-time with 2,840 wins.

In 1937, the Veterans Committee elected McGraw to the Hall of Fame.

CHAPTER 23

FIVE-K RATING

1934 ALL-STAR GAME

July 10, 1934 — New York: The Major League All-Star Game was a new concept in 1934. The first installment of a game that would come to be known as the midsummer classic had been played just the year before at Chicago's Comiskey Park. Many of the same participants were on hand at the Polo Grounds for the rematch, and make no mistake — this was no mere exhibition. The National Leaguers arrived with the game's most dangerous hitters in succession — a quintet of players destined for the Hall of Fame.

Hubbell was also headed for the Hall of Fame, though it was not entirely obvious at the time. After struggling in the minors for six years and giving serious thought to quitting baseball, he had signed with the Giants in 1928 at the relatively advanced age of 25; he would serve the Giants as a player, front-

Carl Hubbell of the Giants, left, and Vernon Gomez of the Yankees, shown before they took the mound as starting pitchers in the All-Star Game in New York City, July 10, 1934.

While Gomez was roughed up for four runs in three innings, Hubbell fanned six very famous hitters in three scoreless frames.

a stated goal: to avenge the previous year's 4-2 setback in front of the 48,368 fans who had gathered to watch.

What they witnessed was an unforgettable moment in baseball history, produced by a left-handed pitcher from Missouri whose screwball ranked among the most baffling pitches of the era. Carl Hubbell would use the pitch on this day to strike out five of

office man and scout for the final 60 years of his life. The slow-delivering southpaw debuted impressively, with a 4-0 shutout of Philadelphia, en route to a 10-6 rookie record. It was the first of 12 consecutive winning seasons.

Hubbell had not won 20 games in a season until 1933, when his 23 victories and 1.66 ERA led the National League, earned him a MVP Award, and sparked the Giants to a World Series title. He also posted 10 shutouts that season, including a remarkable stretch of 46 1/3 consecutive scoreless innings. But Hubbell had struggled enough in his career to know the danger of resting on one's laurels. "A fellow doesn't last long on what he has done," he once said. "He has to keep on delivering."

That's precisely what "King Carl" was aiming to do in 1934, at a time when most Americans were struggling to survive the Great Depression. For many people, baseball offered a sweet respite from the struggles of everyday life. Hubbell's All-Star feat soon became the talk of the land.

To understand the significance of the achievement, try to imagine retiring any one of these American League icons: Babe Ruth, Lou Gehrig, Jimmie Foxx, Al Simmons or Joe Cronin. Just seeing

Hubbell would make history on this day. Charlie Gehringer singled on the first pitch and Heinie Manush drew a walk. Great, Hubbell thought. Two men on, none out — and the great Babe Ruth striding to the plate. If the crowd wanted to see what Hubbell had, his margin for error had just disappeared. The time was now.

Although he was in his last full season, Ruth could still wallop the ball. The Babe had hit 34 homers, second in the AL, just a year before. Naturally, Hubbell was looking for a double-play ball against the 39-year-old slugger, who was none too quick to first base. He tried to get Ruth to chase a fastball out of the zone, but to no avail. So three straight screwballs over the plate followed. Ruth watched every one of them before giving the umpire a perplexed look and returning to the dugout.

Left: Yankee slugger Babe Ruth (left) and Jimmie Foxx (right) of the Philadelphia Athletics, shown in April 1934 at Philadelphia's Shibe Park. Both Ruth and Foxx, among the game's elite hitters, were among Carl Hubbell's strikeout victims in that year's All-Star Game. Right:

Feared right-handed batter Al Simmons, shown here with the Chicago White Sox, won batting titles in 1930 and 1931 by hitting .381 and .390. In 1934, he batted .344 with 104 RBI, but was also among Carl Hubbell's conquests in the All-Star Game.

one of their names on a lineup card was enough to keep a pitcher awake the night before a game. Facing them all in succession was a daunting prospect indeed.

As Hubbell put it, "I can recall walking out to the hill in the Polo Grounds that day and looking around the stands and thinking to myself, 'Hub, they want to see what you've got.'"

The first two batters gave no indication that

Lou Gehrig was next. Unlike his Yankees teammate, this was a power hitter in his prime. He was in the middle of his only Triple Crown season and the second of three home run crowns with a career-high 49 clouts. Having watched the Babe fail to take the bat off his shoulder, Gehrig took a mighty cut at Hubbell's fourth pitch. It was a screwball — strike three!

As Gehrig walked back to the dugout, he

whispered the following advice to Foxx about Hubbell's low-breaking screwball: "You might as well cut. It won't get any higher."

Foxx, the Philadelphia Athletics first baseman, was on his way to 44 home runs, second to Gehrig. He had socked 106 over the previous two seasons, more than any player in baseball. Gehringer and Manush executed a successful double-steal, but Hubbell was unfazed by the baserunning ploy. Catcher Gabby Hartnett kept calling for screwballs, and Foxx went down swinging — on four pitches, just like Ruth and Gehrig.

Striking out those three players successively in a span of 12 pitches, with two men on base, would have ranked among the great athletic feats of that or any era. However, Hubbell was not finished. Al Simmons had won two batting titles in the early 1930s and was

on his way to a .344 season. He struck out to lead off the second inning. And Joe Cronin, the reigning AL doubles champion and a man in the midst of his fifth consecutive 100-RBI season, fared no better. He, too, struck out on the screwball.

Hubbell's feat preceded televised baseball, of course. The lucky 48,368 fans who witnessed the game live, and thousands more who were later entertained by the newsreel in theatres across the country, truly experienced a treat. Although the achievement was hailed by reporters at the time, its status grew exponentially as the years passed by — particularly as the men Hubbell sent on a parade back to the dugout began a parade into the National Baseball Hall of Fame.

HUBBELL'S FEAT IN PERSPECTIVE

Carl Hubbell was known for both his devastating screwball and his remarkable control. During the prime of his career, between 1933 and 1936, he pitched more than 1,200 innings yet walked less than 200 batters. He recorded 10 straight seasons with at least 100 strikeouts, but it was five that did not count on his official pitching record — those historic five in a row during the 1934 All-Star Game — that forever etched his name in baseball history.

Consider the merits of each Hall of Famer he set down on strikes.

Babe Ruth. The most celebrated athlete of his day, Ruth had set a goal of reaching 700 career home runs — a number that was laughable before he came along and changed the game. At the time of the 1934 All-Star Game, he was merely weeks away from getting there. Now in his last full season (and his final year with the Yankees), his power and knack for producing the big hit at the biggest moments kept him among baseball's most feared hitters.

Lou Gehrig. Ruth's teammate and half of the greatest hitting tandem of all time, Gehrig was on his way to winning the 1934 American League Triple Crown. But this man's greatness could hardly be defined by one season. Some called Lou the most valuable Yankee ever for the confidence he brought to the club. And there was plenty of reason for it. For 13 consecutive seasons, he scored 100 runs and knocked in 100 more.

Jimmie Foxx. If the first two were intimidating batters, Hubbell's third strikeout victim was no step down. Foxx, whose muscular arms burst from his sleeves as if to get a head start on pounding the baseball, was nicknamed "The Beast." Jimmie was the second man in history to top 500 career home runs. He had also won the 1933 American League Triple Crown and two straight MVP Awards. He was no easy man to strike out, either, having once walked six times in a game.

Al Simmons. An unusual hitting style that saw him step toward the dugout did not prevent Simmons from finishing his career with more hits than any right-hander in American League history. He was in the middle of his 11th consecutive season with a .300-plus batting average, having won hitting crowns in 1930 and 1931 while helping the Athletics claim pennants in both years. He, too, was considered one of baseball's best clutch batsmen.

Joe Cronin. The smiling Cronin could sure put a frown on a pitcher's face. Known as one of the toughest and most determined hitters of the day, he also had some head on his shoulders, having taken over as Washington's player-manager the previous year. He topped the .300 mark eight times in his career. Skipper Connie Mack once said, "With a man on third and one out, I'd rather have Cronin hitting for me than anybody I've ever seen."

CHAPTER 24

WELCOME TO COOPERSTOWN

HALL OF FAME'S OPENING DAY

June 12, 1939 — Cooperstown, New York: Cooperstown, a quiet village of less than 3,000 nestled on beautiful Lake Otsego between Upstate New York's Catskill and Adirondack mountain ranges, swelled with pride in becoming home to the newest jewel in American sports: the National Baseball Hall of Fame and Museum. Some 15,000 fans and three national radio networks crowded Main Street as 26 inductees, dating to the initial 1936 class, settled into their new home in baseball's proclaimed birthplace.

And what a grand home it is. The two-story building, three years in the making, features walls of James River Colonial brick integrated with stone. Its slate roof, stately pillars, white marble steps and wrought-iron railings comprise a shrine that would not be out of place in any showcase of colonial-era architecture. Just inside, exhibits include the baseball Cy Young pitched for his 500th win in 1910; uniforms donated by Young, Christy Mathewson and Ty Cobb, among others; and a pair of shoes worn for several trots around the basepaths by the great Babe Ruth.

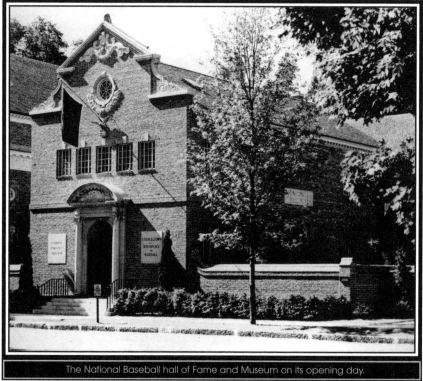

The National Baseball hall of Fame and Museum on its opening day.

"They started something here, and the kids are keeping the ball rolling," Ruth said in his induction speech, shortly before the doors to the Hall of Fame opened. "I hope some of you kids will be in the Hall of Fame. I'm very glad that in my day I was able to earn my place. And I hope youngsters of today have the same opportunity to experience such feeling."

With the opening of the National Baseball Hall of Fame, experiencing the game became easier for children and adults alike. Group after group of fans stood for several minutes at a time in the 1,200-square foot, chandeliered main room before a fireplace, upon which the famed Abner Doubleday baseball sits in a gleaming glass case. Above the mantel is a large oil painting of Doubleday, who, according to a commission appointed by baseball pioneer Albert G. Spalding in 1905, "invented" the game using that very ball 100 years ago.

The Mills Commission spent the better part of three years examining evidence and hearing testimony about the origins of baseball. Abner Graves, an engineer from Denver, lobbied hard in support of Doubleday, a one-time Civil War general who was said to have made significant changes to a game that was called "town ball." Graves said Doubleday used a stick to outline a diamond-shaped playing field in the dirt, and was the man who introduced four bases that led to the name, "baseball." His testimony was convincing. In December 1907, the commission concluded in its final report that "the first scheme for playing baseball, according to the best evidence obtainable to date, was devised by Abner Doubleday at Cooperstown, N.Y. in 1839."

Thus, plans for a grand centennial celebration were set in motion, with the opening of the Hall of Fame as the main event. Of course, Ruth was a big draw. But he was just one of nine inducted players and 12 baseball legends on hand for the ribbon-cutting ceremony, which was presided over by Commissioner Kenesaw Mountain Landis, league presidents Ford Frick (National) and William Harridge (American), and National Association chief William Bramham. Ruth was among the Hall of Fame's star-powered inaugural class, chosen three years earlier by the Baseball Writers' Association of America. Cobb, Mathewson, Walter Johnson and Honus Wagner were the others in the Class of 1936.

Many Americans spent 1939 trying to get back on their feet from the effects of the Great Depression. They did have some colossal entertainment attractions to lift their spirits. Two months after the opening of the National Baseball Hall of Fame, *The Wizard of Oz* premiered in Hollywood. *Gone With the Wind* also debuted before the end of the year, giving 1939 two of the

The excitement over a gathering of this stature was palpable. The "Cavalcade of Baseball" jubilee that had gathered momentum over four months came to a head when Commissioner Landis announced to the crowd, "I now declare the National Baseball Museum and the Baseball Hall of Fame in Cooperstown, New York — home of baseball — open!"

The fans rushed through the Hall of Fame doors. Some had business to take care of outside the Hall's walls as well. The United States Post Office had issued a special, commemorative stamp to mark the day. One million were sold in Cooperstown, with Landis buying the first ones himself. Almost half the stamps issued in Cooperstown were postmarked that very day.

While past greats like Ruth, Cobb, Johnson, Young, Lou Gehrig, Tris Speaker and Nap Lajoie were among the 26 honored for their place in

Ten immortals of the National Game gather at Cooperstown, New York, on June 12, 1939 to celebrate the dedication of the Baseball Hall of Fame. In the front sit (left to right) Eddie Collins, Babe Ruth, Connie Mack, and Cy Young, while in the rear stand (left to right) Honus Wagner, Grover Cleveland Alexander, Tris Speaker, Napoleon Lajoie, George Sisler, and Walter Johnson.

most watched and acclaimed films of all time. To the 25,000-plus fans who passed through the Hall of Fame's doors that year, baseball might have been the biggest blockbuster. And to the lucky ones in Cooperstown for the Hall's opening, nothing could compare.

baseball lore, there were also several current greats putting their skills on display. The inaugural Hall of Fame Game saw Dizzy Dean start for a team managed by Eddie Collins; and Lefty Grove take the mound for a squad skippered by Wagner. For the record, Wagner's team won, 4-2, in a seven-inning game in which players from all 16 Major League clubs participated.

The National Baseball Hall of Fame had become a reality, and that reality matched quite nicely with National League President Frick's vision for it. Earlier that year, Frick had written the following in a letter to the *Spalding Base Ball Guide*: "This is the National Game's Centennial Year, but it will not be a worthy commemoration in the fullest sense unless its influence continues on into the future. Generations to come must know that Base Ball in its hundredth year had high thoughts for the future; that the anniversary observance was not only background by a glamour history but looked forward to greater chapters still to be written, hoping to hand along the fruits of its experience as a heritage to the era yet to be."

Jackie Robinson became the first black player in baseball's Hall of Fame when he was officially inducted and presented with his plaque in Cooperstown, New York, on July 23, 1962.

THE HALL'S FIRST RESIDENTS

A look at the 26 Hall of Famers — four years' worth of honorees — who became immortalized in Cooperstown in 1939:

1936

Ty Cobb:
Longtime baseball hits king retired with .367 average.

Walter Johnson:
Career pitching leader with 110 shutouts.

Christy Mathewson: Won a record 37 games in 1908.

Babe Ruth:
Redefined power hitting with 714 home runs.

Honus Wagner:
Hit .300 or better for 17 straight years.

1937

Morgan Bulkeley:
First National League president.

Ban Johnson
Founder of the American League.

Nap Lajoie:
Hit American League record .426 in 1901.

Connie Mack:
Set managing record with 3,731 victories.

John McGraw:
Skippered 10 pennant and three Series winners.

Tris Speaker:
Rapped a record 792 career doubles.

George Wright:
Revolutionized shortstop position in the 1800s.

Cy Young:
All-time ace is the only 500-game winner in history.

1938

Pete Alexander:
Compiled 373 victories over 20 years.

Alexander Cartwright:
Dubbed "the Father of Modern Baseball."

Henry Chadwick:
Journalist who developed the modern box score.

1939

Cap Anson:
First man to collect 3,000 hits.

Eddie Collins:
His 25 seasons a position-player record.

Charlie Comiskey:
Thrived as player, manager and owner.

Candy Cummings:
Inventor of the curveball.

Buck Ewing:
The dominant catcher of the 1800s.

Lou Gehrig:
Powered Yankees for 2,130 straight games.

Willie Keeler:
Fashioned a 44-game hit streak in 1897.

Charles Radbourn:
"Old Hoss" won 59 games in 1884.

George Sisler:
Set modern record with 257 hits in 1920.

Al Spalding:
Pitcher, sporting goods magnate, organizational genius.

CHAPTER 25

BELTING THE EEPHUS

1946 ALL-STAR GAME

July 9, 1946 — Boston: With the war now a memory, baseball's elite gathered at Boston's Fenway Park for the 1946 All-Star Game — the first midsummer classic in two years. Attendance at major-league ballparks was up about 70 percent in 1946, and American and National Leaguers were particularly giddy over this game. "I don't think I've ever seen a more festive occasion," remarked Yankees manager Bill Dickey about the bird dog that Boston owner Tom Yawkey had given him. Dickey replied that Yawkey had bestowed him with puppies.

During batting practice, Brooklyn's Dixie Walker — who was leading the NL in batting at the time — marveled at Ted Williams' hitting stroke. "Let's take in the sight," Walker said to a

Boston Red Sox slugger Ted Williams follows the flight of the ball after connecting with a Rip Sewell eephus pitch for a home run in the eighth inning of the All-Star Game at Fenway Park in Boston, July 9, 1946.

Phillies first baseman Frank McCormick. "Guys who hadn't seen one another in years were crossing back and forth before the game to shake hands and visit."

This game was so anticipated that additional seating was constructed in Fenway's upper reaches to accommodate 200 members of the media. In the AL dugout, Detroit Tigers ace Hal Newhouser good-naturedly teased Cleveland speedballer Bob Feller about his rumpled suit. While warming up together, Red Sox slugger Rudy York bubbled to New York Times reporter. "Ain't that something? He shore is purty."

Seven other Red Sox were named to the 1946 All-Star Game: York, Dom DiMaggio, Bobby Doerr, Hal Wagner, Dave Ferriss, Mickey Harris, and Johnny Pesky. Yet the 34,906 fans who shoehorned into Fenway Park focused on Williams more than anyone else. In his first four campaigns (1939-42), the Splendid Splinter had rapped a combined .356 and averaged 32 home runs a year, but he missed all of the next three seasons due to the war. While most returning stars had lost their edge, Williams was as sharp as ever in 1946, batting .347 at the All-Star break. In this game, he would bat 1.000 — as well as blast one of the most celebrated home runs in All-Star history.

Williams drew a walk in the first inning and scored on a home run by the Yankees' Charlie "King Kong" Keller. In the fourth, however, Ted struck a big blow, launching a massive drive into the center field bleachers. Williams laced a RBI single in the fifth inning and another single in the seventh, making him 3-for-3 for the day.

The Americans led 8-0 entering the bottom of the eighth, and they still weren't through. Facing Pirates veteran Rip Sewell, the AL made it 9-0 on singles by the Yankees' Snuffy Stirnweiss, St. Louis Browns pitcher Jack Kramer, and the Red Sox'

they wanted the hamburger, then filet mignon, eventually the cow and the entire pasture."

On the hill, Sewell relied partially on a trick pitch called the "eephus" or "blooper" ball. Far more extreme than your typical change-up, the eephus soared skyward — upwards of 20 feet or more — before free falling into the strike zone. Recalled Sewell:

"Before the game, Ted said to me, 'Hey, Rip, you wouldn't throw that damned crazy pitch in a game like this.'

"'Sure,' I said. 'I'm gonna throw it to you.'

"'Man,' he said, 'don't throw that ball in a game like this.'

"'I'm gonna throw it to you, Ted,' I said. 'So look out.'"

When Williams walked to the plate in the

Ted Williams, left, Boston Red Sox outfielder, and Charlie Keller of the New York Yankees laugh in the locker room after the All-Star Game at Fenway Park in Boston on July 10, 1946. The American League beat the National League 12-0.

Vern Stephens. With two on and two out, and Sewell still on the mound, Williams strode to the plate.

Sewell was not your typical ballplayer. He didn't record his first big-league win until age 32; and he didn't serve in the war because part of his foot had been shot off in a 1940 hunting accident. He also was opposed to the burgeoning players' union, saying he was "glad the owners had finally told these ungrateful players where to get off. First

eighth, he shook his head from side to side, meaning don't throw that crazy pitch, Rip. But Sewell, in the jovial spirit of this game, nodded his head. He reared back as if to fire a fastball but instead lobbed an eephus, which Williams fouled off. Sewell nodded and tossed another blooper, but it missed the strike zone and Ted laid off. Rip then snuck a fastball past him for a strike.

"Now I had him one ball, two strikes," Sewell recalled. "I wound up and threw him another blooper, on an arc about 25 feet high. It was a good one. Dropped right down the chute for a strike. He took a couple of steps up on it — which was the right way to attack that pitch, incidentally — and he hit it right out of there. And I mean he hit it."

Williams socked the eephus over the right field fence and into the bullpen, sparking Fenway fans into a frenzy. Sewell chided the Sox slugger throughout his home run trot, and Ted laughed all the way to home plate. Afterward, Sewell made sure everyone knew that this was the first time anyone had ever homered off his eephus.

Williams' blast made the score 12-0, and that's how it ended. The AL used only three pitchers, but together they handcuffed the Nationals on three hits — all singles. Feller allowed two of the hits, Newhouser one, and Kramer zero. Yet all

Rip Sewell, inventor of the "eephus ball," was not your typical player. He did not record his first big-league win until age 32, and did not serve in World War II because part of his right foot had been blown off in a hunting accident.

anyone could talk about was Williams, who finished the day 4-for-4 with two homers, four runs, and five RBI. "That Williams is the greatest hitter of all time!" gushed Tigers manager Steve O'Neill afterward.

Years later, Williams fondly recalled the special day at Fenway in 1946, especially his duel with Rip Sewell. "I got a charge out of that one," he said with a grin. "You should have seen Sewell's face. I had to laugh. I couldn't help it."

BUSINESS IS BOOMING

Throughout the war, Americans spent their evenings huddled around radios, fretting over the distressing news from the European and Pacific Theaters. But the anguish ended in August 1945, and millions celebrated the following year by going to the ballpark. In 1946 attendance figures at major-league stadiums jumped by the highest rate before or since. The numbers below indicate the boom.

American League Attendance

Team	1945	1946	% Increase
Boston	603,794	1,416,944	135%
Chicago	657,981	983,403	49%
Cleveland	558,182	1,057,289	89%
Detroit	1,280,341	1,722,590	35%
New York	881,845	2,265,512	157%
Philadelphia	462,631	621,793	34%
St. Louis	482,986	526,435	9%
Washington	652,660	1,027,216	57%

National League Attendance

Team	1945	1946	% Increase
Boston	374,178	969,673	159%
Brooklyn	1,059,220	1,796,824	70%
Chicago	1,036,386	1,342,970	30%
Cincinnati	290,070	715,751	147%
New York	1,016,468	1,219,873	20%
Philadelphia	285,057	1,045,247	267%
Pittsburgh	604,694	749,962	24%
St. Louis	594,630	1,061,807	78%
MLB Total	10,841,123	18,523,289	71%

CHAPTER 26

JACKIE VOTED NL'S BEST

ROBINSON'S WINNING SEASON

Top: Jackie Robinson in 1945 in his uniform of the Kansas City Monarchs Negro Club. Bottom: Jackie Robinson of the Brooklyn Dodgers, chosen the Most Valuable Player in the National League for 1949, relaxes with his trophies at home in Queens, New York, on November 18, 1949. Robinson, the first black MVP, hit a league-leading .342 for the NL champions, led the league with 37 steals, and scored 122 runs.

Jackie Robinson began the 1949 season as a 30-year-old player entering his third season with the Brooklyn Dodgers. But his story was hardly that of a man his age with just two years of major-league experience.

A unique player of formidable talent, Robinson had carried an unduly heavy emotional load on his shoulders during his first two big-league seasons. By 1949, however — two years after he'd cracked the long-standing color barrier in Major League Baseball — Robinson enjoyed a greater degree of acceptance both on and off the baseball diamond. This change for the better in Robinson's situation was reflected in the extraordinary way he played the game throughout the season.

Although Robinson is regarded as one of the all-time greats of the game, he will always be known first and foremost as a trailblazer for African-American baseball players. Before Robinson came along, a ban on African-American players in the major leagues had stood since the 19th century, when Cap Anson had refused to play with black pitcher George Stovey. This had led to a gentlemen's agreement among baseball owners that blacks were simply not acceptable in the major leagues.

Branch Rickey of the Dodgers thought otherwise. At the end of World War II, he began to send scouts to the Negro Leagues in search of talented players; Rickey did this under the guise that he wanted to field a Negro League team owned by the Dodgers. Hidden under Rickey's stealth blanket was the fact that Rickey was using the exercise to find the perfect player to break the color barrier. Robinson, who played shortstop for the Negro Leagues' Kansas City Monarchs, looked like the right choice.

On October 23, 1945 the wheels of baseball's "Great Experiment" began to turn when Rickey announced the Dodgers' signing of Robinson. A week later, Robinson was assigned to the Montreal Royals of the International League. Based on his speculation that

Opposite: Jackie Robinson crosses home plate on a steal from third as Giants' catcher Walker Cooper (5) fires the ball to third base in an attempt to get the trailing runner. During his career, Robinson stole home 19 times and almost single-handedly re-established daring baserunning as an important component of an increasingly homer-dominated game.

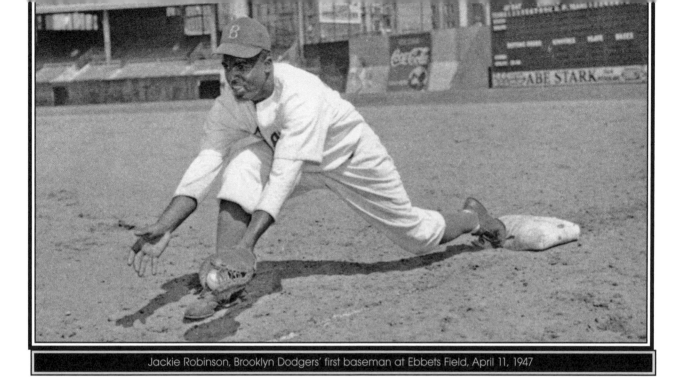

Jackie Robinson, Brooklyn Dodgers' first baseman at Ebbets Field, April 11, 1947

there would be less racial tension in Canada, Rickey thought the placement north of the border would be perfect for Robinson.

During spring training in1946, the Dodgers played their farm team, the Montreal Royals, who had Robinson in the lineup. This game marked the first appearance of an integrated team in 20th century organized baseball.

By joining the Royals, Robinson became the first African-American player to play in the International League in 57 years. He also led the league in batting and runs scored. Robinson's Royals won the pennant by 18 1/2 games and won the Little World Series. Jubilant Montreal fans chased their adored idol for three blocks afterward. Regrettably, there would be less joy greeting Robinson's signing with the Brooklyn

Dodgers in 1947.

During spring training, a petition by Brooklyn players against Robinson was squashed by Dodgers manager Leo Durocher. Still, Rickey kept Robinson at Montreal until just before the start of the season to deflect attention. In fact, it was not announced that Robinson would be joining the Dodgers until the sixth inning of an exhibition game between the Dodgers and Royals, just prior to the start of the 1947 season.

Robinson made his major-league debut April 15, 1947, playing first base. He went hitless but flawlessly handled 11 chances at his new position in a 5-3 Brooklyn win. But Robinson's plight was far more complicated than how he played. In addition to death threats and the many racial insults he heard from the

ROBINSON'S MANY TALENTS

While Jackie Robinson is best known for being the man who broke baseball's color barrier, baseball might not have been his best sport.

Robinson was known as the "Jim Thorpe" of his race because of his talents in many sports. While at UCLA he became the school's first four-letter man. As a halfback on the Bruins' football team, Robinson averaged an amazing 11 yards per carry as a junior and was heralded widely as the best running back in America. On the basketball court his skills were equally impressive as he led the Pacific Coast Conference in scoring during his junior and senior seasons.

After those performances, Robinson received a healthy dose of the real world where racism still existed

to a large extent. Despite being the Conference scoring champion each of those seasons he was not named to the first, second, or third all-conference teams.

Track brought out additional talents in the Robinson skill set as he won the 1940 NCAA long-jump title and was a shoe-in for the 1940 Olympics had not World War II cancelled the Games.

Robinson also won a national Negro tennis tournament and he competed in swimming at UCLA and won several championships.

Baseball became the final sports destination for Robinson, but it's clear he would have excelled in just about any athletic endeavor he decided to pursue.

stands, Robinson endured racism in other ways; on the road, he had to stay at different hotels and eat at different restaurants than those of his white teammates. And there was the rumored strike by the St. Louis Cardinals in response to playing against a black player — and the baiting game played by the Philadelphia Phillies manager. But Robinson kept his head held high and his mouth shut, as he had agreed to do when Rickey talked about bringing him aboard.

All of the abuse endured by Robinson served to galvanize the support he received from his teammates. In addition, every black man, woman, and child suddenly became a Dodgers fan.

other major-league team rosters.

On the field, Robinson was superb in 1949. His 13th inning home run gave the Dodgers a 2-1 win over the Giants at the Polo Grounds on May 30. That year's All-Star Game at Ebbets Field on July 12 featured the first appearance of black players in the midsummer classic. The National League lineup included Robinson, Roy Campanella, and Don Newcombe, while Larry Doby was among the American League stars. But the high point of Robinson's season came on July 28, when he completed a 12-for-25 run that moved his batting average to .364. A game best for Robinson followed

Robinson and wife Rachel receive a new car presented by dancer Bill Bojangles. Robinson on Jackie Robinson Day, Sept. 23, 1947. The car, a gift from fans, is part of the celebration of the newly clinched National League Championship.

Rickey and Robinson had opened the door for black players in organized baseball. Others followed during the 1947 season, like Dan Bankhead, who pitched for the Dodgers, Larry Doby with the Cleveland Indians, and Hank Thompson and Willard Brown with the St. Louis Browns.

Rickey only imposed a one-year silence on Robinson. Once liberated, Robinson became a different player and person. He became more aggressive on the field and started speaking out on racial issues away from the field. By 1949 he began to show that he didn't mind protesting a blown call by the umpire. Nor did he mind voicing his opinion about the conspicuous absence of black players from

on September 20, 1949, when he stole home for the fifth time that season — his 13th time since coming to the major leagues. At that point, only Ben Chapman had stolen home more, having done it 15 times — in 11 seasons.

At the end of the season, Robinson led the National League with a .342 batting average, along with 37 stolen bases. On November 18, 1949, Robinson was selected as the National League's Most Valuable Player. While Robinson would go on to be elected to the Hall of Fame, his performance in 1949 firmly established that black players deserved to play in the major leagues.

CHAPTER 27

JOE AND MARILYN

THE SLUGGER AND THE SEX SYMBOL

On their honeymoon in February 1954, Marilyn Monroe and Joe DiMaggio stopped in Korea, where Marilyn entertained American troops with 10 shows in four days. More than 100,000 lusting males hooted and whistled at the curvaceous beauty, who appeased them with sexy dresses, seductive smiles, and photo ops for a lucky few.

Back at the hotel, Marilyn reportedly gushed, "Joe, Joe, it was wonderful. The troops loved me. You have never heard such cheering."

Retorted her miffed husband, a nine-time World Series champion, "Yes, darling, I have."

It was perhaps inevitable that the marriage of baseball's greatest living icon and America's most desirable sex symbol would fail. Joe DiMaggio, insecure in relationships as it was, could not share his wife with the rest of the world.

DiMaggio and Monroe, each of whom was divorced, first met at Toots Shor's saloon in Manhattan in early 1952. Like every other man with a pulse, Joe fell fast and hard for Marilyn. Yet when asked what it was like to date the blond bombshell, DiMaggio had tersely replied, "Better than rooming with Joe Page."

Monroe, who had grown up without a father, appreciated the strength, experience, and paternalistic kindness of her much older beau. The couple dated for about a year before marrying in San Francisco's City Hall on January 14, 1954. Marilyn wore a brown wool cocktail suit with a white mink collar, as well as a platinum eternity band that sparkled with 35 baguette-cut diamonds. An army of photographers swarmed around the beaming couple, who appeased them with a passionate kiss.

Right from the start, however, many predicted that the marriage wouldn't last. DiMaggio was 39 years old, retired, and from an Italian culture in which women stayed home and catered to the family. In contrast, the 27-year-old Monroe was rocketing to superstardom. Her biggest role to date had been in the 1953 film *Niagara* — famous for her scenes in a smoking-hot red dress.

DiMaggio's frustration and jealousy boiled over on September 15, 1954. Monroe was filming her famous skirt-blowing scene for *The Seven Year Itch* on New York's Lexington Avenue. Hundreds of gawkers delighted in the risque spectacle, but director Billy Wilder recalled seeing "the look of death" on DiMaggio's face. The following month, Monroe officially separated from DiMaggio on October 5. Citing "mental cruelty," she divorced him three weeks later.

Lois Weber Smith, Monroe's press agent, tried to explain what went wrong: "For a while, when they were married, Marilyn had the idea she could have both lives, the private and the public. She deceived herself in that ... It was almost as if Marilyn Monroe and Joe DiMaggio met at the wrong time in their lives."

Monroe went on to star in Hollywood blockbusters, and she married playwright Arthur Miller. But tragedy followed: two miscarriages, divorce, admittance to a psychiatric hospital, and ugly rumors of affairs with John and Robert Kennedy.

DiMaggio despised all of Marilyn's hangers-on — including the Kennedys — and remained deeply in love with her. In the early 1960s they were back together, with DiMaggio trying to help her through her personal difficulties. But rumors of a possible remarriage abruptly ended on August 5, 1962, when Monroe died alone from an overdose of sleeping pills.

Blaming them for her death, DiMaggio barred Hollywood types from Monroe's funeral, which he oversaw. For the next 20 years, Joe had a half-dozen red roses delivered to her crypt three times a week. He never remarried.

Marilyn Monroe and Joe DiMaggio share a kiss on their wedding day, January 14, 1954. They were united in San Francisco after a year-long courtship, but their marriage lasted only nine months.

Opposite: Newlyweds Joe DiMaggio and Marilyn Monroe arrive at the San Francisco International Airport, January 29, 1954, with plenty of baggage prior to their departure for Tokyo for an extension of their honeymoon. They were married in San Francisco on January 14. Marilyn is under suspension by her studio for failing to start a new picture.

CHAPTER 28

THE MICK DONS THE TRIPLE CROWN

MANTLE'S SHINING SEASON

Top: Mickey Mantle, New York Yankees outfielder, lays down a bunt and practices breaking from the plate in his first workout with the club, March 2, 1954 in St. Petersburg, Florida. The young flychaser, always a superb bunter, is digging in with his right leg — the one on which he had just undergone a serious operation. Bottom: Mickey Mantle of the Yankees and Ted Williams of the Red Sox carry the weapons that made them famous prior to a doubleheader, July 4, 1956 at Boston's Fenway Park. Mantle led the AL in homers four times, while Williams remains the last batter to hit .400 in a season.

Mickey Mantle had the name, the looks, the ability and the label — the burdensome tag of unlimited potential.

A strapping youngster from Commerce, Oklahoma, Mantle was a switch-hitter with amazing power from both sides of the plate who could run like few players in major-league history. Scouts marveled at their stopwatches that timed Mantle from the left side of the plate to first base in 2.9 seconds: a clocking that defied the geometry of the game.

Branch Rickey called Mantle the best prospect he'd ever seen. And prior to Mantle's arrival to the major leagues in 1951, New York Yankees manager Casey Stengel said of his whiz kid: "He should lead the league in everything. With his combination of speed and power he should win the triple batting crown every year. In fact he should do everything he wants to do."

Except play shortstop. He'd made far too many errors in the minor leagues to play shortstop in the majors, particularly when the Yankees had future Hall of Famer Phil Rizzuto playing the position. So when the Yankees broke camp in 1951, Mantle was the team's right fielder.

Mantle's skills caught everyone's attention from the outset. Early in the 1951 season he walloped a 450-foot home run. But the power display didn't eradicate his troubles hitting major-league pitching. So he was sent back to the Yankees' minor-league affiliate in Kansas City for further seasoning.

After some soul searching, Mantle regained his confidence and joined the Yankees for good in August. During Game 2 of the 1951 World Series, Mantle tripped over an exposed drainpipe in Yankee Stadium's right center field. In doing so he tore cartilage in his knee and missed the rest of the World Series. Sadly, the injury kicked off what would be a career wrought with injury.

Mantle returned to the lineup in 1952, moving to center field to replace the retired Joe DiMaggio. Despite his many physical gifts, Mantle was not the new DiMaggio in the minds of Yankees fans, who seemed to take delight in reminding him of that fact.

Opposite: New York Yankees manager Casey Stengel, left, crowns his center fielder Mickey Mantle, the winner of the 1956 Triple Crown. The two posed prior to the 1956 World Series. Mantle's .353 batting average, 52 home runs, and 130 runs batted in established him as the seventh player in major-league history to top all three categories in one season.

New York Yankee center fielder Mickey Mantle connects for a single against the Kansas City Athletics at Yankee Stadium on June 6, 1956. The pitcher in this circumstance is none other than Tommy La Sorda, who later managed the Los Angeles Dodgers.

However, Mantle could do some things even the great DiMaggio could not. He hit a 565-foot home run at Washington's Griffith Stadium in 1953. Mantle's home run prompted Yankees pitcher Bob Kuzava to observe, "I never saw a ball hit so far. You could have cut it up into 15 singles."

May 13, 1955 brought another memorable Mantle centerpiece when he hit three home runs at Yankee Stadium, each surpassing the 461-foot sign.

Still, the total package expected from Mantle's "unlimited potential" label haunted him until 1956, when everything came together for one memorable summer at the ripe old age of 24.

Mantle entered May with four homers under his belt. He then exploded, hitting 16 for the month to put him 11 games ahead of Babe Ruth's pace when Ruth set the season home run record with 60 in 1927. As if the number of home runs hit during the month were not enough, Mantle put an exclamation point on the month of May, during a May 30 doubleheader

CROWN JEWELS

The Triple Crown is awarded to the hitter who leads his own league in home runs, batting average, and runs batted in (RBI). The three categories must be led or tied at the end of the season in order to be part of a Triple Crown performance. Here's how Mickey Mantle's 1956 Triple Crown season stacks up against the other Triple Crown winners in major league history:

American League

Year	Player	HR	AVG	RBI	Team
1887	Tip O'Neill	14	.435	123	St. Louis
1901	Nap Lajoie	14	.426	125	Philadelphia
1909	Ty Cobb	9	.377	107	Detroit
1933	Jimmie Foxx	48	.356	163	Philadelphia
1934	Lou Gehrig	49	.363	165	New York
1942	Ted Williams	36	.356	137	Boston
1947	Ted Williams	32	.343	114	Boston
1956	Mickey Mantle	52	.353	130	New York
1966	Frank Robinson	49	.316	122	Baltimore
1967	Carl Yastrzemski	44	.326	121	Boston

National League

Year	Player	HR	AVG	RBI	Team
1922	Rogers Hornsby	42	.401	152	St. Louis
1925	Rogers Hornsby	39	.403	143	St. Louis
1933	Chuck Klein	28	.368	120	Philadelphia
1937	Joe Medwick	31	.374	154	St. Louis

against the Washington Senators at Yankee Stadium.

Facing Pedro Ramos in the fifth inning of the opening game, Mantle swung at a 2-2 pitch and the ball took off like a rocket toward right field, nearly clearing the roof. If the ball had risen approximately two feet higher, Mantle would have owned the distinction of being the first player to ever hit a fair ball out of Yankee Stadium.

Afterward the dimensions of Yankee Stadium were examined by careful scrutiny of the historic park's blueprints. It was determined that Mantle's drive hit the roof some 370 feet away from home plate, at a point 117 feet above ground level. Mantle claimed the blast was the best he'd ever hit left-

Due to a pulled groin muscle, Mantle did not start the final game of the season, but Stengel kept tabs on Kaline's progress. Kaline entered the final day of the season with 126 RBI to Mantle's 129. Stengel's plan was to pinch-hit Mantle in the event Kaline got close. And he did.

So in the ninth inning Stengel put a bat in Mantle's hands. Mantle grounded out to score Jerry Lumpe from third and boost his RBI season tally to 130; Kaline finished the day with two RBI for a season total of 128.

Mantle won the Triple Crown and the MVP, batting .353 with 52 homers and 130 RBI in one of the best all-around seasons ever. In addition to those

MICKEY MANTLE'S TITANIC 565-FOOT HOME RUN
HIT RIGHT-HANDED, FIFTH INNING, AGAINST WASHINGTON SENATORS, CHUCK STOBBS PITCHING. GRIFFITH STADIUM, APRIL 17, 1953

This photo shows the path of Mickey Mantle's titanic 565-foot home run. Hitting right-handed, Mantle clubbed the prodigious blast in the fifth inning off the Washington Senators' Chuck Stobbs at Griffith Stadium, April 17, 1953.

handed.

He added his 20th home run of the season in the second game and a drag-bunt single just for show.

At the end of the doubleheader Mantle led the major leagues in runs (45), hits (65), total bases (135), runs batted in (50), batting average (.425), and home runs (20). Talk of Mantle winning baseball's coveted Triple Crown began to gain real steam at this point.

By the end of the season, the Yankees were well on their way to the American League pennant. The only remaining suspense stemmed from Mantle's pursuit of the Triple Crown, with Detroit's Al Kaline creeping up in the RBI race.

lofty numbers, he led the American League with 132 runs scored and a .705 slugging percentage — only the ninth man in baseball history to exceed .700.

In a city where Willie Mays and Duke Snider played for the New York Giants and Brooklyn Dodgers, respectively, Mantle reigned as the top center fielder and player in baseball. Legions of New York youngsters would grow up holding Mantle in high esteem as their hero. Though Mantle enjoyed a Hall of Fame career, the injuries and his propensity for the night life kept him from enjoying future seasons like the one he'd enjoyed in 1956 — a season regarded as one of the best put together by any player in the history of the game.

CHAPTER 29

WILLIE'S HOME RUN DERBY

GOING FOR THE RECORD

April 30, 1961 — Milwaukee: Talk about an athlete. Willie Mays owned every possible skill a baseball player could possess. He could run, hit for average, hit for power, field, and throw. Contemporary baseball vernacular would have called Mays a "five tool" player.

When he joined the National League's New York Giants in 1951 at age 20, he already had plenty of professional baseball experience dating back to age 16, when he played for the Birmingham Black Barons of the segregated Negro Southern League. Once he

major leagues reflected one of the positive changes. Jackie Robinson had been the perfect guy to break the color barrier in 1947. Given his phenomenal skills, which set him apart from any one who'd ever played baseball, Willie Mays was the perfect guy to show everyone what the game had been missing. No less than the great Joe DiMaggio touted Mays' arm as the best in baseball history. And one baseball scribe put Mays' ability in perspective when he wrote, "Willie Mays should play in handcuffs to even things up."

Willie Mays (24) follows through after connecting for his fourth homer of the game on April 30, 1961, in Milwaukee. His eighth-inning shot against the Braves in Milwaukee made Mays one of 15 major-league players to hit four home runs in a single game. The Braves catcher is Hawk Taylor (26) and the umpire is Chris Pelekoudas.

graduated from high school, the Giants signed Mays and he quickly advanced to the Giants' top farm team in Minneapolis, Minnesota, where he was playing when Giants manager Leo Durocher gave him the call to the Polo Grounds in New York City.

Post-World War II America was quickly changing and the advent of the black baseball player in the

Playing with the Giants, Mays quickly thrust himself into the national spotlight. He showcased his abilities to all in the first game of the 1954 World Series, when he raced to the center wall with his back to home plate to make an over-the-shoulder catch of Vic Wertz's drive. The Giants swept the 1954 Series and Mays' catch became the memento most carried in their minds when recalling that Fall Classic.

While Mays could chase down any ball hit, he had few peers at the plate. And the "Say Hey Kid" put on a hitting display in Milwaukee against the Braves on April 30, 1961 that few players in major-league history have equaled.

The Giants had made a cross-country move from New York to San Francisco in 1958; a move that was tough on Mays. He "owned" New York City, but had to start over with the West Coast fans. Playing in the Pacific time zone also made his exploits harder to follow for a national audience. But his performance against the Braves reminded everyone about the player he was.

A crowd of 13,114 showed to watch the Giants-Braves game on Mays' special day.

Entering the game, the Giants found themselves in the midst of a power surge having hit five home runs in the previous day's game. But Lou Burdette would be starting for the Braves and he had other

for the season.

Any time a slugger of Mays' stature got out of the gate quickly, the "what ifs" followed. No doubt many of those in attendance were already thinking about the possibility of Mays matching the major-league record of four home runs in one game. Cleveland's Rocky Colavito had been the last player to turn the trick when he did it in 1959 — and became just the eighth player in major-league history to do so. Joe Adcock of the Braves had been the last National Leaguer to hit four in one game when he did so in 1954. Others in the stands were likely counting the number of at-bats Mays might get. Could Mays actually hit five home runs if he got five at-bats?

Such thoughts suffered a setback, however, in the fifth inning. Burdette had been chased after three innings, so when Mays stepped into the batter's box for his third at-bat, he looked at right-hander Moe Drabowsky. The crowd came to life in anticipation. Could he? Would he?

Giants outfielder Willie Mays proudly displays the four baseballs, representing the four homers he hit against the Milwaukee Braves on April 30, 1961 at Milwaukee County Stadium. Willie's homers accounted for eight runs batted in. In 1961, Mays finished second in the NL with 40 homers and third in RBI with 123.

ideas for the Giants' bats.

Intents and purposes aside, Burdette didn't exactly have his way with the Giants center fielder. Mays greeted the veteran pitcher with a solo home run in the first inning to put the Giants up 1-0. Burdette faced Mays again in the third — and once again had to watch as Mays deposited one of his pitches over the fence to double his home run total

Evoking a collective groan from the grandstands, Mays lined out to center field. Trailing 7-3, the Braves had inserted pitcher Seth Morehead into the game — their fourth pitcher of the day — prior to Mays' fourth at-bat in the sixth inning. And the slugger connected for his third home run. Despite the lopsided score of 11-4 after seven innings, nobody was about to leave Milwaukee's County Stadium until they saw Mays get his fifth at-bat.

When Mays walked to home plate in the eighth inning, every fan in the ballpark cheered for him to achieve baseball immortality against the Braves' sixth pitcher of the game, Don McMahon. One swing of the bat and Mays could walk with Colavito, Adcock, Lou Gehrig, Gil Hodges, Pat Seerey, Chuck Klein, Ed Delahanty, and Bob Lowe, the others who had achieved the feat.

Mays delivered, hitting his fourth home run of

Rocco Domec "Rocky" Colavito, shown here in 1967 with the Cleveland Indians, is one of 15 men to hit four homers in one game. One of the great power hitters of the sixties, Colavito connected for four long balls on June 10, 1959 for the Indians against the Baltimore Orioles.

the game. The crowd roared while simultaneously counting the remaining outs. What would take to bring Mays to the plate for one last at-bat in the ninth inning?

The countdown continued until one hitter separated Mays from a sixth at-bat. With two outs in the ninth inning, Mays advanced to the on-deck circle with Jim Davenport hitting. Once again the crowd roared — if only the mighty "Say Hey Kid" could get one more swing at baseball immortality. But that glorious opportunity never materialized. Davenport grounded out to end the Giants' ninth.

When most baseball fans think about Willie Mays' Hall of Fame career, they reminisce about the extraordinary basket catches he made in the outfield. Or how his hat would fly off as the "Say Hey Kid" sped around the bases. Yet one of Mays' most memorable achievements came that April day in 1961, when he hit four home runs in one game.

THE FOUR-HOMER CLUB

When Willie Mays hit four home runs in one game, he became the ninth major leaguer to do so. Here's a look at the eight who accomplished the feat before Mays.

May 30, 1894: Bobby Lowe
Boston Beaneaters, NL

July 13, 1896: Ed Delahanty
Philadelphia Phillies, NL

June 3, 1932: Lou Gehrig
New York Yankees, AL

July 10, 1936: Chuck Klein
Philadelphia Phillies, NL

July 18, 1948: Pat Seerey
Chicago White Sox, AL

August 31, 1950: Gil Hodges
Brooklyn Dodgers, NL

July 31, 1954: Joe Adcock
Milwaukee Braves, NL

June 10, 1959: Rocky Colavito
Cleveland Indians, AL

April 30, 1961: Willie Mays
San Francisco Giants, NL

Of these players, Gehrig and Adcock came the closest to hitting a fifth home run. Gehrig, who hit his home runs in consecutive at-bats, hit a deep fly ball in his last at-bat that nearly cleared the fence, while Adcock sandwiched a double off the top of the wall among his four home runs.

Meanwhile, Delahanty is an abnormality among these players as one or all of his home runs were inside-the-park home runs, depending on which account you read. He is the only player on the list with any inside-the-park home runs among his four. Here's a look at the players who followed Mays by hitting four in one game:

April 17, 1976: Mike Schmidt
Philadelphia Phillies, NL

July 6, 1986: Bob Horner Atlanta Braves, NL

September 7, 1993: Mark Whiten
St. Louis Cardinals, NL

May 2, 2002: Mike Cameron
Seattle Mariners, AL

May 23, 2002: Shawn Green
Los Angeles Dodgers, NL

September 25, 2003: Carlos Delgado
Toronto Blue Jays, AL

LEGENDARY
MOMENTS

CHAPTER 30

TODAY...TODAY...TODAY...

THE IRON HORSE SAYS GOODBYE

Top: New York Yankees first baseman Lou Gehrig, who has taken himself out of the lineup, watches his teammates warm up prior to their May 2, 1939 game against the Detroit Tigers at Briggs Stadium. The Yankees won 22-2. Bottom: Babe Ruth, Yankees immortal, embraces longtime teammate Lou Gehrig on July 4, 1939 at Yankee Stadium. Gehrig was almost too moved to speak to the 60,000 fans gathered to honor him, but delivered an emotional and memorable speech that has lived on in baseball lore.

July 4, 1939 — New York: Lou Gehrig's roommate, Bill Dickey, had seen indications that his friend was ill. He saw Gehrig's legs buckle for no apparent reason. He observed Gehrig having difficulty bending down to tie his shoelaces. He saw his fingers shake.

Still, neither Dickey nor the rest of the baseball world was prepared for the stunning announcement from the Mayo Clinic that Gehrig had been diagnosed with the terminal illness amyotrophic lateral sclerosis — in lay terms, chronic infantile paralysis. Gehrig was only 36 years old. He was the "Iron Horse" of baseball, having set a record by playing in 2,130 consecutive games, a span that lasted almost 14 years.

In the days following the June 21 announcement of Gehrig's diagnosis, the Yankees quickly organized a tribute for their fallen star, despite Gehrig's protests. The ceremony, which was to include a reunion of the 1927 world champion Yankees, was planned for July 4, between games of a doubleheader against Washington at Yankee Stadium.

"There hasn't been a day since I came up that I wasn't anxious to get in uniform and out on the field," Gehrig said that day. "But today I wish I was anywhere but in this stadium."

Packing Yankee Stadium to pay tribute to their hero, more than 61,000 fans disagreed with Gehrig. As soon as the first game ended, Captain Sutherland's Seventh Regiment Band opened the 40-minute ceremony. The old-timers joined Gehrig in a parade to the flagpole in center field, where the 1927 world championship flag was raised. The team then assembled around home plate, where Gehrig received many trophies and other gifts.

Among the gifts was a large silver trophy, about 18 inches tall with a wooden base, supported by six silver bats with an eagle atop a silver baseball. The trophy was a gift from his teammates, whose names appeared on one side. On the other was a poem, composed by a writer for *The New York Times*, John Kieran, at the request of the Yankees players.

Opposite: Lou Gehrig, the "Iron Horse" of the New York Yankees, wipes away a tear during a sold-out tribute at Yankee Stadium July 4, 1939. Gehrig's record-breaking career was cut short by neuromuscular disease. He later died on June 2, 1941.

Lou Gehrig became a New York City parole commissioner on Oct. 11, 1939, by appointment of Mayor Fiorello LaGuardia.

As Yankees President Edward Barrow presented Gehrig with the trophy, Gehrig came to tears and many in the crowd thought he was on the verge of collapsing. Gehrig appeared so overcome with emotion that he might not be able to address the crowd, but he finally found another dose of his indomitable will and stepped toward the microphone.

After expressing his appreciation to his former and current teammates and to the Yankees organization, Gehrig once again thrust himself into baseball immortality with these words:

"What young man wouldn't give anything to mingle with such men for a single day as I have for all these years. You've been reading

DISSECTING THE STREAK

During Lou Gehrig's streak of playing in 2,130 consecutive games, there were numerous times when the streak could have ended, including only a month after the streak began. On July 5, 1925, Gehrig did not start the game but was inserted into the lineup later.

On April 23, 1933, he was knocked unconscious by a pitch from Washington's Earl Whitehall, but recovered and stayed in the game.

On June 14, 1933, Gehrig and Yankees manager Joe McCarthy were thrown out of a game at Boston for arguing an umpire's call. McCarthy received a three-day suspension but Gehrig was not suspended. Six weeks later, on July 26, 1933, Gehrig was again thrown out of a game, in the second game of a doubleheader.

On May 10, 1934, Gehrig left the game against the White Sox after five innings, suffering from a severe cold, but was back in the lineup the following day.

On June 29, 1934, he was beaned while playing in an exhibition game and suffered a concussion but still remained in the lineup.

The most serious threat to his consecutive game streak occurred on July 13, 1934. Suffering from what was diagnosed as lumbago, Gehrig had to be helped off the field after the first inning in a game at Detroit because of the severe pain in his back. The streak stood at 1,426 games and most observers thought it would end at that point.

The next day, however, the Yankees found a way for the streak to continue by moving Gehrig into the leadoff spot in the batting order. After he led off the game with a single and managed to reach first base, he was removed for a pinch runner. He recovered in time to play again the next day.

On June 8, 1935, Gehrig was involved in a collision at first base with Boston's Carl Reynolds in the first game of a doubleheader and had to leave the game with an arm and shoulder injury. He came back and played in the second game.

On Aug. 5, 1935, Gehrig suffered another lumbago attack in his back and was forced to leave a game against the Red Sox in the fourth inning. He was back in the lineup for the following game.

On May 2, 1939, the streak finally ended when Gehrig benched himself because he didn't believe he was helping the team with his subpar performance.

about my bad break for weeks now. Yet today, I consider myself the luckiest man on the face of the earth … I might have had a bad break, but I have an awful lot to live for."

When Gehrig finished, his friend and teammate, Babe Ruth, came to stand beside him and said something that produced a laugh. As the band played, "I Love You Truly," the crowd took up the chant, "We love you Lou," as Gehrig and teammates made their way off the field.

After a few moments of rest, Gehrig returned to the dugout for the second game of the doubleheader; he would serve the rest of the season as the team's inactive captain. Long after that game had ended, he and his former roommate, Dickey, left the stadium together.

"Bill, I'm going to remember this day for a long time," Gehrig said.

Gehrig's streak had begun when the 22-year-old native New Yorker appeared as a pinchhitter for Peewee Wanninger on June 1, 1925 and singled. The following day, with regular Wally Pipp complaining of a headache, manager Miller Huggins put Gehrig into the starting lineup at first base. That was where he stayed for the next 14 seasons.

Always playing in the shadow of his more famous and boisterous teammate, Ruth, Gehrig quietly became one of the greatest players in the history of the game. His streak continued through a broken thumb, a broken rib, a broken toe, a twisted back, colds, lumbago and headaches. He was a career .340

hitter and drove in 100 or more runs for 13 consecutive years. His 493 homers, third only to Ruth and Jimmie Foxx on the career lists when he retired, included a record 23 grand slams.

Gehrig started the 1939 season slowly, and realized something was wrong. After a game against Washington on April 30, Gehrig made up his mind that he needed to come out of the lineup. He told manager Joe McCarthy, and the streak ended on May 2, when Gehrig sat out the Yankees' game at Detroit.

When his condition had not changed a few weeks later, Gehrig went to the Mayo Clinic to be examined, and received the stunning news.

Gehrig once said that he "was not a headline guy." He would have preferred crowds cheer for stars such as the young John Wayne in *Stagecoach* or for the opening of *Gone With the Wind* or the New York World's Fair. He did not want people coming to a special ceremony

New York City Mayor Fiorello LaGuardia, standing at right of the microphones, pays his respects to Lou Gehrig, left, as 60,000 fans jammed Yankee Stadium on July 4, 1939 to cheer the retiring "Iron Horse." The World Champions paid tribute to their great first baseman during their doubleheader with the Washington Senators. The two teams are shown in the infield, with the famous 1927 Yankees team in the foreground, in a row at right. Dignitaries and a band are in the background.

to honor him or to acknowledge him with what he considered undeserved accolades.

McCarthy was one of the speakers saluting Gehrig that day, and he could barely control his emotions.

"It was a sad day in the life of everybody when you told me you were quitting because you felt you were a hindrance to the team," the manager said. "My God, man, you were never that."

CHAPTER 31

THE SHOT HEARD 'ROUND THE WORLD

THOMSON'S GIANT HIT

Top: Bobby Thomson of the New York Giants picks out one of his bats for the World Series opener against the New York Yankees at Yankee Stadium on Oct. 4, 1951. Bottom: Bobby Thomson of the New York Giants hits one of the most famous home runs in baseball history. This homer, hit in the bottom of the ninth against the Brooklyn Dodgers at the Polo Grounds in New York City, October 3, 1951 not only won the game but also the National League pennant for the Giants.

October 3, 1951 — New York: It's not surprising that the Speedy Alka-Seltzer character premiered in 1951. The news of the day made stomachs churn. Not only did war rage in Korea, but a zealous General MacArthur was pushing American troops toward China, sparking fears — said President Harry Truman — "of World War III." Moreover, the U.S. was nearing completion of a hydrogen bomb, a thousand times more powerful than the atomic bomb dropped on Hiroshima. The "Red Scare" was so tangible that New York City purchased 2.5 million I.D. bracelets for schoolchildren so that their remains could be identified in case of a Soviet nuclear strike. All New Yorkers could say was, "Thank God for baseball."

Never before (or since) has one city enjoyed so much exciting baseball as New York did in 1951. Each of the Big Apple's three major-league teams boasted a superstar center fielder — Willie Mays of the New York Giants, Mickey Mantle of the New York Yankees, and Duke Snider of the Brooklyn Dodgers. From Coney Island to Manhattan, the trio was known collectively as "Willie, Mickey, and the Duke."

In 1951 the Yankees had won two straight World Series and were cruising to their third consecutive pennant. In the National League, the Dodgers — a perennial contender — seemed destined for another Subway Series matchup with the Yankees. Some had thought that the Giants would make a run, but in July Dodgers manager Charlie Dressen declared, "The Giants is dead." Indeed, on August 12, Brooklyn held a 13 game lead over their rival.

Nevertheless, the Giants and their fans weren't about to give in to the hated Dodgers. Their rivalry was so intense, noted sportswriter Bruce Lowitt (only half jokingly), that "people got knifed over who was a better pitcher, Carl Erskine or Sal Maglie." The Giants and Dodgers were the only teams in major-league history to play in the same city, the same league, and at the same time. They faced each other more than 20 times a year — half in Brooklyn's quirky Ebbets Field (with such offbeat fans as bell-ringing Hilda Chester) and half in the Giants' mammoth Polo Grounds.

Opposite: Manager Leo Durocher, left, of the New York Giants, has a big hug for third baseman Bobby Thomson after Thomson's three-run, ninth-inning homer topped the Brooklyn Dodgers, 5-4, on October 3, 1951. The win, which came in the clubs' third and deciding playoff game, gave the Giants the National League pennant, climaxing New York's flag drive, which began in earnest in mid-August.

Bobby Thomson of the New York Giants homers at the Polo Grounds against the Brooklyn Dodgers to win the clinching playoff game, October 3, 1951. Ralph Branca is the Dodger pitcher who has just served up the home run ball.

The Dodgers, immortalized in Roger Kahn's book *The Boys of Summer*, boasted the most talent of the two clubs, including Hall of Famers Roy Campanella, Snider and Jackie Robinson. Yet the Giants were getting career years from Monte Irvin (121 RBI) and Bobby Thomson (32 homers), while Sal Maglie and Larry Jansen were on their way to career highs in wins (23 apiece). Moreover, the rookie Mays — after a 1-for-25 career start had brought him to tears—sparked the Giants with his dynamic bat, glove, and speed.

With all guns firing, New York was nearly unbeatable down the stretch. Manager Leo "The Lip" Durocher led the Giants to an incredible 37-7 finish and a final record of 96-58. On the season's final day, the Dodgers were the team that seemed "dead." They needed a three-run rally in the eighth and a Robinson home run in the 14th to defeat the Phillies and tie the Giants for first place.

According to the rules of the time, the two first-place teams would play each other in a three-game playoff, with the winner playing the Yankees in the World Series. New Yorkers were ecstatic; exactly three major-league teams had reached the postseason, and each was from the Big Apple! City Hall proclaimed it

DREAM PARKS

In baseball as in theater, drama has much to do with setting. In 1951 the atmosphere at Ebbets Field and the Polo Grounds enlivened the Giants-Dodgers rivalry and made the playoff climax that much more exciting.

Built on the former Pigtown garbage dump, Ebbets Field in Brooklyn was a cozy, quirky ballpark. In right field, which was of lower elevation than center, stood a wall and scoreboard that jutted out in numerous directions. A slugger could win a suit if he hit the Abe Stark sign in right. On the Schaefer Beer sign, either the h or the e would light up depending on whether a questionable play was judged a hit or an error. Cowbell-ringing Hilda Chester and the Dodgers Symphony Band were among the characters who rooted for "Dem Bums."

At the Polo Grounds, only pull hitters had a prayer of reaching the fences. The center field wall was 505 feet from home plate, while a hitter needed just a 280-foot pop to left field or a 257-foot poke to right to begin a home run trot. The outfield sloped so much that Giants manager Leo Durocher could see his center fielder only from the waist up. The Polo Grounds is where the term hot dog was coined (for food, not a cocky ballplayer), and where 90,000 boxing fanatics turned out for a Jack Dempsey bout in 1923.

When Thomson cracked his "Shot Heard 'Round the World," team broadcaster Russ Hodges went hoarse screaming "The Giants win the pennant!" eight times. Newsreel shows fans grabbing their heads in delirium and shaking their arms to the heavens. Fans lingered around the Polo Grounds for hours afterward, savoring the sweetest moment of their New York lives.

"Baseball Week in the World's Greatest City."

As it turned out, Bobby Thomson would be the center of attention. Although dwarfed in popularity by Willie, Mickey, and the Duke, Thomson had put up impressive numbers in the postwar years, clubbing 25 homers or more four times. He played in two All-Star Games, and some said he was the fastest baserunner in the league. In Game 1 of the playoffs at Brooklyn (the first game ever broadcast on radio coast to coast), Thomson's two-run homer keyed a 3-1 Giants victory. In Game 2 at the Polo Grounds, however, he made a baserunning blunder and two errors, as the Dodgers romped 10-0.

It all came down to Game 3. Across New York, workers gathered around radios while pedestrians huddled in front of storefront windows to watch the

The Giants, though, still weren't "dead." Alvin Dark and Don Mueller opened the bottom of the ninth with singles, and after a Monte Irvin foul-out, Whitey Lockman laced a double to left, scoring Dark. With runners on second and third and one out, and the score 4-2, Dressen replaced Newcombe with Ralph Branca.

A man who scoffed at symbols of bad luck, Branca wore No. 13 and posed with black cats. But perhaps he had tempted fate too long, for on a 0-1 pitch, Thomson blasted a low line drive deep to left. Thomson remembered every detail:

"At first I was sure it was a home run," he recalled. "Then I saw the ball start to sink when I got halfway to first. I look again, and I realized it was disappearing into the stands. Then I knew we were all right. I jumped and skipped around the bases like I was half-nuts. 'Gee

New York Giants players and fans converge on Bobby Thomson, whose head is being rubbed, after his pennant-winning, three-run home run in the ninth inning of the third playoff game with the Brooklyn Dodgers at the Polo Grounds in New York October 3, 1951. Running in from the left is teammate Ed Stanky. Trying to get to Thomson is Manager Leo Durocher (hatless, third from left).

game on television. Even at Rikers Island, prisoners were allowed to listen to the historic matchup. Under overcast skies, pitcher Don Newcombe and the Dodgers held a 1-0 lead until the bottom of seventh, when Thomson tied the score with a sacrifice fly.

In the eighth, the Dodgers rallied for three runs, scoring on a wild pitch and singles by Andy Pafko and Billy Cox. Entering the bottom of the ninth, Brooklyn's 4-1 lead seemed so secure that the PA announcer informed sportswriters to pick up their World Series passes in the Dodgers' clubhouse after the game.

whiz!' I kept saying, 'Gee whiz!'"

The Giants mobbed Thomson at home plate while radio announcer Russ Hodges described the scene: "The Giants win the pennant! The Giants win the pennant! And they're going crazy! Oh-ho!"

While the Korean War continued throughout 1951, the threat of world war diminished and no H-bombs were dropped. Instead, the most immortal blast of the year — at least in the hearts of Giants fans — was Bobby Thomson's "Shot Heard 'Round the World."

CHAPTER 32

AN ALL-STAR MEMORY

1955 ALL-STAR GAME

July 12, 1955 — Milwaukee: Milwaukeeans loved their baseball. Back in 1953, the Braves' first season in Beer City after relocating from Boston, Milwaukee had set a National League attendance record (1,826,397). Spirits at the ballpark ran high each year in the mid-1950s, as the Braves were an annual pennant contender. But this game was something new and exciting: for the first time ever, such stars as Mantle, Mays, Williams, and Musial gathered in America's dairyland to put on a show for over 45,000 fans in Milwaukee's County Stadium — the host of the 1955 Major League All-Star Game.

Yet as fans settled into the bleachers to see baseball's greatest heroes in action, there was a somber was delayed a half-hour out of respect for the late "In the Wake of the News" columnist.

But once the 22nd annual midsummer classic got under way, however, there was nothing remotely somber about the riveting exhibition game, as dramatic as anything concocted by Hollywood. The lucky fans in Milwaukee's County Stadium thrilled to terrific performances by the Braves players, long blasts by the famous sluggers, an amazing catch by the New York Giants' Willie Mays, a come-from-behind effort by the home team, and a dramatic home run in extra innings to end it. Even Yankees catcher Yogi Berra would contribute a memorable quote. To borrow the slogan of

Stan Musial of the St. Louis Cardinals has just broken up the 1955 All-Star Game at Milwaukee's County Stadium with a 12th-inning homer. He is being congratulated by Phillies pitcher Robin Roberts (wearing a Milwaukee Braves jacket).

Other NL stars, including Gil Hodges of Brooklyn (#14) and Ernie Banks of the Cubs (between Roberts and Hodges) follow in close pursuit. The NL's 6-5 win was its first since the 1949 contest.

undercurrent to the festivities on this sun-splashed day in southwest Wisconsin. That morning, many of baseball's elder statesmen had gathered in Chicago to pay their final respects to legendary *Chicago Tribune* sportswriter/promoter Arch Ward. A "Damon Runyonesque" character in the sports world, known for his superhuman work ethic and spiffy wardrobe, Ward had created the All-Star Game in 1933 for the Windy City's "Century of Progress" Exposition. Today, just three days after Ward had suffered a fatal heart attack at the age of 58, the start of the 22nd All-Star Game

Old Milwaukee beer, "It doesn't get any better than this."

Early on, it looked like the American League was on its way to a rout. Harvey Kuenn, a Wisconsin native, led off with a hit and moved to third on a single to right center field by scrappy Nellie Fox of the White Sox. Kuenn then scored on a wild pitch from Phillies workhorse Robin Roberts. After Boston legend Ted Williams walked, Yankees wunderkind Mickey Mantle launched a towering blast that landed in Perini's woods behind center field. The Americans had scored four runs with nobody out.

Ironically, the AL would score only one more run. In the sixth inning, Berra scored following a double by young Tigers phenom Al Kaline and a groundout by old-reliable Mickey Vernon of the Washington Senators. Meanwhile, NL hitters couldn't crack AL pitchers Billy Pierce (the diminutive White Sox lefty) and Early Wynn (the Indians burly right-hander). Through six innings, the American League led 5-0. That's when the excitement began.

In the seventh inning, Williams belted a long drive to right center. But the spectacular Mays, who had made the most famous catch in history in the previous fall's World Series, soared above the barrier to rob the Splendid Splinter of a home run.

The Say Hey Kid wasn't through. In the bottom of the seventh against crafty Yankees lefty Whitey Ford, Mays led off with a single. After two fly-outs, 21-year-old Hank Aaron of the hometown Braves strode to the plate. For the future home run king, who would be named to 21 All-Star teams, this was his very first at-bat in a midseason classic. He cajoled a walk, putting

major-league history. Now, pitching in his first All-Star Game, he struck out pitcher Ford to end the inning.

Ford retired the first two men in the bottom of the eighth before surrendering another single to Mays. Muscle-bound Ted Kluszewski of the Reds and "Handsome" Ransom Jackson of the Cubs followed with singles, scoring Mays and closing the gap to 5-3. Frank Sullivan, a six-feet-seven-inch-tall Red Sox right-hander, came in to face Aaron. Unfazed, Hammerin' Hank ripped a single to right. When Kaline's throw got away from Al Rosen at third, Jackson chugged home with the tying run. The score was tied, 5-5.

That's the way it remained through the next three innings. Both teams couldn't cash in on scoring chances in the ninth. Nuxhall walked the first batter in the 10th, then struck out the side. In the bottom of the 10th, Sullivan allowed a hit, but fanned two.

In the top of the 11th, with two outs and men on the corners, Cardinals second baseman Red Schoendienst saved a run. He snagged a Berra grounder up the middle and then threw him out on a bang-bang play at first. Yogi gave umpire Dusty Boggess a mouthful

Nearly obscured by overjoyed teammates, Stan Musial crosses home plate after slamming the first pitch of the 12th inning over right field screen for the game-winning homer in Milwaukee on July 12, 1955. A three-time MVP, Musial would hit .319 in 1955 (third among NL hitters) and club 33 home runs.

men on first and second. The next batter, fiery Braves shortstop Johnny Logan, brought the locals to their feet with a Texas league single, scoring Mays. When shortstop Chico Carrasquel flubbed a Stan Lopata grounder, Aaron scored to make it 5-2.

The AL loaded the bases in the eighth, prompting NL skipper Leo "The Lip" Durocher to summon Joe Nuxhall from the bullpen. Eleven years earlier, a 15-year-old Nuxhall had become the youngest pitcher in

before giving up the fight. The Nationals went down 1-2-3 in the 11th, setting the stage for the historic 12th.

Gene Conley of the Braves took the hill in the top of the 12th inning. A year earlier, the quiet, six-feet-seven-inch-tall right-hander had lost the game for the NL. Yielding three runs in a third of an inning, he had retreated to the dressing room in tears. "I goofed up out there," he had said. "I was terrible." This time, though, Conley looked like Cy Young. He struck out all three men he faced — batting champions Kaline and Vernon and home run champ Rosen. Conley walked back to the dugout amid a thunderous standing ovation.

Leading off the bottom of the inning, Stan Musial dragged himself to the plate. The revered, 34-year-old Cardinals star had played every frame of this marathon game. So too had Berra, who prepared for his 12th inning in the afternoon sun.

"I'm tired," Musial remarked to Berra.

"So what?" Yogi shot back. "I'm tired, too. We're all tired."

Stan Musial's unusual left-handed batting style led some observers to say that he hit as if he were peeking around the side of a building. He batted over .300 17 times, which included 16 consecutive seasons.

And with that, as if granting a favor to Berra, Musial ended the game. On the first delivery from Sullivan, Stan the Man belted a waist-high pitch into the sun-drenched bleachers in right field. County Stadium erupted in cheers as the National Leaguers prevailed, 6-5.

That day, some lucky fan left the ballpark with one of the most famous home run balls in All-Star history. Virtually everyone went home happy. Aaron had gone 2-for-2. Logan had knocked in a run. Conley had struck out the side. The superstars had lived up to their billing. And the home team had won. It was a great day for baseball, a great day to be alive. Arch Ward would have been proud.

ALL-STAR THEATRICS

In each July during the 1950s, while finding refuge in air-conditioned movie theaters, millions of Americans witnessed the spectacle of the All-Star Game on newsreel. Stan Musial's blast in 1955 may have been the most famous All-Star clout of the decade, but several other big-leaguers emerged as heroes in the midsummer classic — most frequently Willie Mays.

In the 1950 All-Star Game at Chicago's Comiskey Park, Ted Williams broke his elbow in the top of the first inning, yet he played and still went 1-for-4. The score was tied, 3-3, through nine innings, and remained so until the 14th. In the top of that frame, Cardinals second baseman Red Schoendienst — who had sat for 10 innings — bashed a game-winning home run for the National League.

Down 9-8 at Cleveland in 1954, the American League rallied for three in the bottom of the eighth, thanks in part to a home run by the Indians' Larry Doby — prompting a roar from 68,000 fans. Musial could have pushed the NL ahead with a two-run homer in the ninth, but two of his long blasts veered foul. In the 1956 All-Star Game, Musial, Williams, Mickey Mantle, and Mays all homered. But Cardinals third baseman Ken Boyer stole the show with three hits and a trio of spectacular plays at the hot corner.

The Giants' Mays played in 24 midsummer classics and holds numerous All-Star Game records. In 1957 his triple in the bottom of the ninth almost helped the NL pull out a victory. Two years later, the "Say Hey Kid" laced a three-bagger in the bottom of the eighth — this once pushing across the winning run in a 5-4 NL triumph. Mays' incredible playing skills later prompted Ted Williams to say, "They invented the All-Star Game for Willie Mays."

CHAPTER 33

SWEET PERFECTION

1956 WORLD SERIES, GAME 5

October 8, 1956 — New York: Autumn 1956 was one of the most turbulent periods of the decade. The Suez Canal crisis brewed in Egypt, while citizens of Hungary rebelled against Soviet rule, prompting a harsh crackdown by the USSR that left thousands dead. Much to Americans' relief, President Dwight Eisenhower kept the U.S. out of both imbroglios. In fact, on October 3, Ike and Secretary of State John

presence at Brooklyn's Ebbets Field. Ike greeted ballplayers, posed for photographs, and threw out the first ball. Dodgers reserve Don Zimmer recalled the thrill of these Yankees-Dodgers matchups. "I called myself a professional cheerleader," he said. "It was a tremendous time. It was something very special."

Yankees pitcher Don Larsen, however, didn't share all of Zimmer's enthusiasm. Larsen had grown

New York Yankees catcher Yogi Berra leaps into the arms of pitcher Don Larsen, who has just fanned Brooklyn Dodgers pinch hitter Dale Mitchell to complete a perfect game. The milestone came in Game 5 of the World Series at Yankee Stadium on October 8, 1956. It is the only no-hit game in World Series history.

Foster Dulles played hooky to take in Game 1 of the World Series.

New York buzzed with excitement for yet another Subway Series. The Yankees and Brooklyn Dodgers had played each other in three fall classics over the previous four years, with Brooklyn winning its first world title in 1955. The 1956 meeting seemed particularly exciting, due in part to Eisenhower's

up on the opposite coast, in California, and took an odd route to New York. He had gone 7-12 as a St. Louis Browns rookie in 1953 and 3-21 for the Baltimore Orioles in 1954. And although he posted records of 9-2 and 11-5 for the Yankees in 1955 and 1956 (thanks largely to New York's powerhouse lineup), he hardly boasted the golden boy stature of such teammates as Mickey Mantle and Whitey Ford.

In fact, Larsen was a hulking, slouched-shoulders presence on the mound. Late in the 1956 campaign, he had to adopt a no-windup delivery because, with it, batters were detecting whether he was throwing a fastball or a curveball. Though Larsen was tough to hit that season, he struggled to find the plate, averaging an alarming 4.8 walks per game.

Although he started Game 2 of the 1956 World Series in Brooklyn, Larsen was so wild — allowing four walks and four runs — that manager Casey Stengel yanked him in the second inning. With the series tied at two games apiece, Stengel announced that Larsen would start the critical Game 5. Yankees reporters and fans grumbled about the decision. Even Larsen wondered if his skipper had made the right call. "After what I did in Brooklyn, he could have forgotten about me, and who would blame him?" he said.

Though Game 5 would be an early afternoon affair, Larsen stayed out until midnight the night before, drinking several beers. Perhaps it helped him forget about the importance of the next day's task and the star-studded lineup he would face: Roy Campanella, Duke Snider, and Jackie Robinson, just to name the future Hall of Famers.

To the 64,619 spectators for Game 5, Larsen seemed composed and nonchalant. Not once did he wave off Yogi Berra's signs; he just reared back and threw, with uncharacteristic precision. In the top of the first, he rang up the first two batters, Junior Gilliam and Pee Wee Reese, on called third strikes. And through four innings, he was perfect — 12 up, 12 down.

The Dodgers appeared to solve Larsen in the fifth, but Gil Hodges' blast to left center was backhanded by Mickey Mantle (whose fourth-inning homer had put New York up 1-0). And an apparent home run by Sandy Amoros hooked just foul. After Amoros

grounded out to end the inning, Larsen breezed through the sixth with two pop-outs and a strikeout. Incredibly, he still had a perfect game — no hits, no walks, no runners reaching base.

The Yanks moved ahead 2-0 in the bottom of the sixth, and in the seventh the crowd gasped with every Larsen pitch. The scene was eerie, with a smoky haze hanging in the air and the late afternoon shadows looming ever larger. Leading off the seventh, Gilliam almost grounded a base hit, but shortstop Gil McDougald made a fine play to gun him down. Larsen then retired Reese and Snider to end the frame.

During the bottom of the seventh, Larsen stepped into the runway area of the Yankees' dugout for a quick drag of a cigarette. Spotting Mantle, he said, "Do you think I'll make it, Mick?" Mantle was startled. In baseball, when a pitcher has a no-hitter going, you don't talk to him — especially when it's a perfect game in the World Series.

This was as close as the Brooklyn Dodgers came to getting a hit in the fifth World Series game at Yankee Stadium, New York, October 8, 1956. At top left, a hot second-inning bouncer off Jackie Robinson's bat glances off the glove of Yankees third baseman Andy Carey. Yanks shortstop Gil McDougald, backing up play, top right, fielded the deflected ball and threw to first baseman Joe Collins just in time to beat Robinson.

The ever-dangerous Jackie Robinson opened the eighth by tapping to the mound. Hodges followed with a low liner to the left of third baseman Andy Carey, but he snatched it inches off the ground, eliciting a roar from the monstrous crowd. Amoros then flied out to Mantle to end the inning.

When Larsen came to bat in the bottom of the eighth, fans showered him with a Ruthian-style ovation. Maglie struck out the side, but no one seemed to notice.

In the top of the ninth, Larsen was so nervous that, as he said later, "I thought I was going to faint." Somehow, he got Carl Furillo to fly out to left. The next batter, Campanella, "hit a drive that I was sure would be a home run," Larsen said. "But it curved foul at the last second. I was so nervous, I almost fell down. My legs were rubbery, and my fingers didn't feel like they were on my hand. I said to myself, 'Please help me out, somebody.'"

That someone was McDougald, who fielded a Campanella grounder cleanly and threw him out. Now one out from a perfect game, Larsen faced pinch hitter Dale Mitchell. The crowd groaned as the first pitch was outside, but roared on the next two: a slider for a strike and a swing and a miss. Mitchell prolonged the tension with a foul into the stands. With the count 1-2, Berra called for a fastball, and Larsen responded by blazing a heater on the outside corner. Mitchell stood frozen while umpire Babe Pinelli thumbed him out.

Yogi Berra, the New York Yankees legendary catcher, is shown here in a 1956 photo. Three times, Berra was named the AL's Most Valuable Player, and he finished second in the voting twice more. He helped the Yankees win the 1956 World Series by hitting .360 in the seven games with three home runs and ten RBI.

Yankee Stadium erupted in bedlam. Berra ran to the mound and jumped into his pitcher's arms. His teammates buried him in hugs. Don Larsen had achieved the ultimate pitcher's fantasy: a perfect game in the World Series. The Yankees would win Game 7 to clinch the title, but what everyone remembers is Larsen's masterpiece, which many still hail as the greatest moment in baseball history.

HOW HE DID IT

Larsen's perfect game, inning by inning:

- First: Larsen strikes out Junior Gilliam and then Pee Wee Reese on called third strikes. Duke Snider lines out to Hank Bauer in right field.

- Second: Jackie Robinson lines one off third baseman Andy Carey's glove; shortstop Gil McDougald grabs the ball and throws him out. Gil Hodges strikes out and Sandy Amoros pops out to Billy Martin at second base.

- Third: Carl Furillo flies out to right field, Roy Campanella fans, and pitcher Sal Maglie lines out to Mickey Mantle in center field.

- Fourth: Gilliam and Reese ground out to second base. Snider takes a called strike three.

- Fifth: Robinson flies out to right field, and Mantle makes a terrific backhanded grab of a Hodges smash to left center. After hooking an apparent home run just foul, Amoros bounces out to second base.

- Sixth: Both Furillo and Campanella pop out to Martin. Maglie strikes out.

- Seventh: McDougald robs Gilliam of a groundball hit. Reese flies out to center field and Snider flies out to left field.

- Eighth: Robinson bounces out to Larsen, and Hodges rips a low liner that's caught by Carey. Amoros flies out to Mantle.

- Ninth: Furillo flies out to LF. Campanella's apparent home run ball curves foul, and he grounds out to second base. Pinch hitter Dale Mitchell, on a 1-2 count, takes a called strike three.

CHAPTER 34

CALIFORNIA, HERE WE COME

TEARS IN MUDVILLE

For fans of New York's three major-league teams, 1957 turned out to be the baseball equivalent of "annus horribilis" (Latin for "horrible year"). Not only did the Yankees lose the World Series to the Milwaukee Braves — the Big Apple would lose two

men said nothing had been decided.

"At this time I wouldn't say that we would go," Stoneham noted, while O'Malley said the owners' approval only allowed the "exploration of further possibilities."

An era ends. Dusty Rhodes of the New York Giants is thrown out at first base for final out in the Giants' last game at the legendary Polo Grounds in New York City, September 29, 1957. The San Francisco-bound Giants lost to the Pittsburgh Pirates, 9-1, in the finale, which drew 11,606 mourners.

of its teams to sunny California by year's end.

Two names became "mud" in the eyes of heartbroken New Yorkers. Both Giants owner Horace C. Stoneham and Dodgers owner Walter F. O'Malley had led fans to believe that there was still a chance the clubs would return to New York. At a May meeting in Chicago, when their fellow owners had cleared the way for a Giants move to San Francisco and a Dodgers move to Los Angeles, both

By August, it was clear that the Giants would be heading west as California's first major-league team. The club's board of directors voted 8-1 in favor of the move on August 19. The reason was clear. While the team had drawn well over a million fans during their 1954 championship season, the 1956 season brought just 629,000 spins at the stadium turnstiles. The support in 1957 had been only slightly better.

"I feel bad for the kids," Stoneham told a *New York Journal-American* reporter. "I've seen lots of them at the Polo Grounds, but I haven't seen any of their fathers lately." The early announcement at least allowed fans to bid their heroes farewell. Several former players were among the 12,000 who witnessed a 9-1 Giants loss to the Pirates on September 29. After the game, fans tore up the field and took home everything they could carry. In addition to souvenirs, most carried heavy hearts.

"It would have broken John's heart," sighed Blanche McGraw, the widow of the longtime Giants manager. "The Giants have been my life."

Brooklyn fans could certainly sympathize. "Dem

day, its residents cried different tears just two years later, on October 8, when the worst-kept secret in baseball became official. O'Malley was taking the Dodgers to Los Angeles, where a 50,000-seat stadium was planned.

O'Malley's team was still drawing more than a million fans a year, but Ebbets Field — opened in 1913 — was showing its age; a campaign to build a new park in downtown Brooklyn had long ago stalled. In a final game that no one knew for sure would be the last, just 6,702 were there to see the Dodgers blank Pittsburgh 2-0.

Ten days later, Brooklyn — the borough, not the team — cried in unison, as many did again three

A young Dodgers fan waves a banner at Ebbets Field as the Brooklyn Dodgers defeat the Philadelphia Phillies, 7-3, in Brooklyn, N.Y., Sept. 22, 1957. A crowd of 6,662 persons attended the Dodgers' second-to-last game at Ebbets Field. The following season, the Dodgers began playing in Los Angeles.

Bums" had frustrated their die-hard supporters for years, but during that magical summer of 1955, the Dodgers had finally pulled through against the hated Yankees. If an entire borough shed tears of joy that

years later when their beloved field was demolished. "When they tore down Ebbets Field," said Dodgers great Duke Snider, "they tore down a little piece of me."

CHAPTER 35

BETTER THAN PERFECT

HADDIX'S NEAR MISS

May 26, 1959 — Milwaukee: In retrospect, Harvey Haddix perhaps should have stayed home on this fateful night. The small, boyish-looking left-hander had a lousy cold, and the Milwaukee weather — chilly with storm clouds looming — was doing him no good. "The Kitten" should have been on a couch snuggled under a blanket, but instead, he took to the hill, hoping to pitch enough good innings for Pittsburgh to earn a win against the

looked forward to an easy win. Their ace, Lew Burdette — a 20-game winner the year before — was on the mound, and the reigning NL-champion Braves boasted one of the most powerful offenses in baseball. Hank Aaron and Eddie Mathews would go on to set the major-league record for home runs by teammates (eclipsing even Babe Ruth and Lou Gehrig's total), while Joe Adcock owned the MLB record for most total

Pittsburgh Pirates Harvey Haddix throws one of his 12 perfect innings against the Milwaukee Braves, May 26, 1959, in Milwaukee. Haddix was perfect through 12, but ended up losing the game in the 13th, 1-0. No other pitcher in baseball history has thrown 12 perfect innings in a game.

Braves.

The 19,194 fans who flocked to Milwaukee County Stadium hoped for a short, quick victory. Some probably even wondered why the game was scheduled in the evening, since this was the middle of the work week (Tuesday) as well as a school night. Nevertheless, fans

bases in a game with 18 (four homers and a double).

Haddix himself had won 20 games, but that was way back in 1953. Ever since, he had struggled to pull his weight. Pitching in the big leagues isn't easy when you stand just five-feet-nine-inches-tall and rely on a fastball and slider. Only by changing speeds and hitting his spots was Haddix able to win 43 of his 87 decisions from 1955 through 1958. This game appeared to be another big challenge for the 33-year-old hurler, especially since Braves manager Fred Haney loaded the lineup with seven right-handed batters.

Fortunately for Haddix, his control was razor sharp. He pitched 1-2-3 innings in the first and second, and a leaping grab by Pirates shortstop Dick Schofield of a Johnny Logan liner helped keep the Braves off the bases in the third frame. Showing no effects from his cold, Harvey pitched a perfect fourth and fifth as well.

What amazed Milwaukee pitcher Bob Buhl was that the Braves hitters knew what was coming. "His catcher, Smoky Burgess, was tipping them off," Buhl recalled. "Burgess was chubby and couldn't squat all the way down . . . We'd yell from the bench what he was calling. But Harvey was doing such a good job of putting on and

trying to go from first to third on an infield single.

A chilly rain fell in the seventh inning, but Haddix — a military veteran — steeled himself against the elements. He retired the side in order in the seventh and eighth, eliciting a standing ovation from the rival crowd. Well-informed fans knew that a perfect game (meaning 27 up, 27 down) had been thrown only three times during regular-season play in major-league history. Excluding Don Larsen's perfecto in the 1956 World Series, no one had achieved the feat since Charlie Robertson did it in 1922.

Desperate to score for their pitcher in the top of the ninth, the Pirates cracked two hits, but Bob Skinner lined out to first baseman Adcock with a man on third. In the bottom of the ninth, Haddix fanned Andy Pafko, got Logan to fly to left, and struck out Burdette. Harvey had done his part to pitch a perfect game, but with the

Harvey Haddix shakes the hand of Milwaukee Braves slugger Joe Adcock on May 27, 1959, in Milwaukee. The night before, Adcock had broken up Haddix' no-hitter in the 13th inning with a game-winning double.

taking off speed that the hitters couldn't time him."

Logan almost spoiled the perfect game in the sixth inning when he bounced one between short and third. But Schofield again came to the rescue, snatching the grounder and gunning out Logan with a long throw. Unfortunately for Haddix, the Pirates remained scoreless against Burdette, despite a steady barrage of singles. Pittsburgh should have scored in the third with their three hits, but Roman Meijas was thrown out

score 0-0, he was forced to go to extra innings.

At this point, Milwaukee's fans had clearly changed sides. The Braves could win any day, but a perfect game was something fans could tell their grandkids about. Incredibly enough, Haddix breezed through the 10th, 11th, and 12th without allowing a runner. No one had ever pitched more than 11 innings of no-hit ball, let alone a perfect game for that long. After each inning, fans encouraged Harvey with raucous standing Os.

Meanwhile, a still-strong Burdette mowed down the Pirates in the 13th. In the bottom of the frame, it wasn't Haddix but his defense who finally broke down. Braves defensive replacement Felix Mantilla, leading off the 13th, chopped a routine ball to Don Hoak at third base. Hoak had plenty of time to get the runner, but he bounced the ball off first baseman Rocky Nelson's knee. Since the play was scored an error, the no-hitter remained — although the perfect game was gone. "I'll never forget that play," Haddix recalled. "Hoak had all night after picking up the ball. He looked at the seams . . . then threw it away."

After Mathews sacrificed Mantilla to second, Haddix intentionally walked Aaron to set up a potential double play. That's when Adcock ruined everything. Honing in on a hanging slider, Adcock blasted the pitch to deep center field. Bill Virdon retreated to the fence, but it sailed over. Aaron thought the ball had fallen short of the barrier — and with Mantilla already across the plate with the winning run — stopped running. Adcock unintentionally passed Aaron on the bases and thus was called out, his apparent homer ruled a double. Regardless, the Braves won 1-0, ruining Harvey's perfect game, no-hitter, and shutout all in a matter of minutes.

Milwaukee Braves right-hander Lew Burdette was the winning pitcher against Harvey Haddix on May 26, 1959. Burdette, winner of 203 major-league games, including a career-best 21 in 1959, threw 13 shutout innings, allowing 12 hits but no walks.

After the game, Burdette was among the many who offered condolences to Haddix, saying "you pitched the greatest game that's ever been pitched in the history of baseball." Yet none of the platitudes eased the pitcher's misery. He felt sick, and it had nothing to do with his stupid cold.

"Harvey didn't even go to bed that night," remembered teammate Elroy Face. "He just walked the streets until sometime in the morning." In an interview 15 years later, Haddix admitted he hadn't gotten over the 13-inning heartbreaker. "It still hurts," he said. "It was a damn silly one to lose."

BOX SCORE OF THE NEAR-PERFECT GAME

County Stadium
Milwaukee, Wisconsin
May 26, 1959
PIT: 000 000 000 000 0
MIL: 000 000 000 000 1

Pittsburgh

	AB	R	H	RBI
Dick Schofield SS	6	0	3	0
Bill Virdon CF	6	0	1	0
Smoky Burgess C	5	0	0	0
Rocky Nelson 1B	5	0	2	0
Bob Skinner LF	5	0	1	0
Bill Mazeroski 2B	5	0	1	0
Don Hoak 3B	5	0	2	0
Roman Mejias RF	3	0	1	0
Dick Stuart PH	1	0	0	0
Joe Christopher RF	1	0	0	0
Harvey Haddix P	5	0	1	0
Totals	47	0	12	0

Milwaukee

	AB	R	H	RBI
Johnny O'Brien 2B	3	0	0	0
Del Rice PH	1	0	0	0
Felix Mantilla 2B	1	1	0	0
Eddie Mathews 3B	4	0	0	0
Hank Aaron RF	4	0	0	0
Joe Adcock 1B	5	0	1	1
Wes Covington LF	4	0	0	0
Del Crandall C	4	0	0	0
Andy Pafko CF	4	0	0	0
Johnny Logan SS	4	0	0	0
Lew Burdette P	4	0	0	0
Totals	38	1	1	1

Pittsburgh

	IP	H	R	ER	BB	SO
Harvey Haddix (L)	12.2	1	1	1	1	8

Milwaukee

	IP	H	R	ER	BB	SO
Lew Burdette (W)	13.0	12	0	0	0	2

Doubles: Adcock. Sacrifice hits: Mathews. Double plays: Milwaukee 3. Errors: Hoak. Left on Base: Pittsburgh 8, Milwaukee 1.

Attendance: 19,194. Time of game: 2:54.

CHAPTER 36

WILLIAMS' LAST HURRAH

SO LONG, SPLENDID SPRINTER

September 26, 1960 — Boston: "All I want out of life," Ted Williams said early in his career, "is that when I walk down the street folks will say, 'There goes the greatest hitter who ever lived.'"

Beginning in 1939, and throughout the 1940s and 1950s, the Boston Red Sox left fielder pursued his quest. He ripped .406 in 1941, topped .340 in 11 seasons, and led the league in slugging and on-base percentage a combined 21 times. Williams was serious and focused. He detested sportswriters and

baseball legacy, he volunteered for combat in World War II and the Korean War. In Korea, he flew 39 combat missions and amazed his fellow Marines with his skill and courage. He was a true American hero, more so than the patriotic movie actors of the day. As author Robert Lipsyte noted, "[He] was what John Wayne would have liked us to think he was."

In 1959 Williams hit under .317 for the first time ever, finishing at .259. He was so disgusted

Red Sox slugger Ted Williams crosses home plate at Boston's Fenway Park after homering in the eighth inning of the club's final home game of the 1960 season on September 28. It was William's 521st home run and came in the last at-bat of his career. Sox catcher Jim Pagliaroni, the next batter, welcomes Williams home.

all their rumors and gossip. Instead, he was a man of pride, honor, and grand ambitions, in the mold of Ernest Hemingway and Theodore Roosevelt.

On newsreels in America's movie theaters, Williams looked larger than life as he launched majestic home runs and circled the bases in workmanlike fashion. At the expense of his

that when the season ended, he demanded that Boston cut his salary from $125,000 to $90,000. Ted could see the writing on the wall. The following year, 1960, would be a new decade, his fourth in the Majors. He would turn 42 on August 30. In 1960, fellow war hero Dwight Eisenhower would serve his final year as president before passing the torch to a youthful John F. Kennedy.

Williams made it clear that 1960 would be his final season. And although his body was literally falling apart — a pin held his collarbone together — Williams played with characteristic pride. Entering the final home game of the season, he was batting .316 with 28 home runs.

The home finale at Fenway Park was on a cold, dreary Wednesday afternoon, and the Red Sox were some 30 games out of first place. After this day's matchup against Baltimore, the Sox were scheduled to head to New York for the season's final series. Williams, though, had other ideas.

"I had had it, and I knew it," he said. "I had gone as far as I could. When I arrived at the park that day, I said to [manager] Higgins, 'Mike, this is the last game I'm going to play. I don't want to go to New York.'" Higgins said he didn't have to.

Prior to the game, the Red Sox paid tribute to

earned a raucous ovation from the small crowd. Not surprisingly, the man of honor limited his response to three sentences, although he expressed his gratitude.

"If I were starting over again and someone asked me where is the one place I would like to play," he said, "I would want it to be in Boston, with the greatest owner in baseball, Tom Yawkey, and the greatest fans in the America. Thank you."

By game time, the fans didn't realize that this was Williams' final contest. His prospects for the game didn't look good, either; it was drizzling, the wind was blowing in, and a lefty sinkerballer, Steve Barber, stood on the hill for the Orioles. In the first inning, Ted walked on four pitches. In the third, against right-hander Jack Fisher, he flew out to center.

Moments later, the press box announcer stated that Williams' immortal No. 9 would be retired by

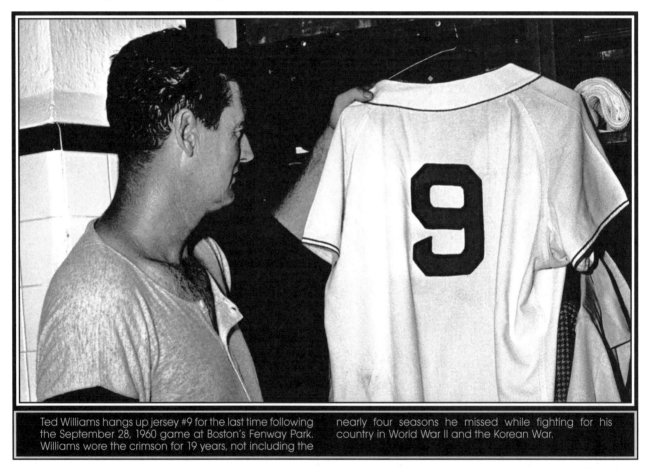

Ted Williams hangs up jersey #9 for the last time following the September 28, 1960 game at Boston's Fenway Park. Williams wore the crimson for 19 years, not including the nearly four seasons he missed while fighting for his country in World War II and the Korean War.

Williams with a small ceremony. They awarded him a plaque and a silver bowl; Boston Mayor John Collins presented a check in Ted's honor to the Jimmy Fund, a charity for children with cancer. Announcer Curt Gowdy introduced Williams, who

the Red Sox after the game. Reporters took this to mean that Williams wasn't going to New York — that this was his very last game.

Thus, each of Williams' remaining at-bats became precious. In the fifth inning, Ted blasted a

Opposite: Ted Williams, right, chats with Cy Young in 1951.

128

Fisher fastball high and deep to right center field. "I hit the living hell out of that one," he would say later. "I really stung it." However, the cold, the wind, and the heavy air kept the ball in the park, with right fielder Al Pilarcik hauling it in at the wall nearly 400 feet away.

By the bottom of the eighth, it was frigid and dark; the lights were on. The Red Sox trailed 4-2, and it appeared that Williams' at-bat that inning would be his last. Fans began to cheer as Ted walked to the on-deck circle. When he stepped into the box, the crowd rose to its feet.

Facing Fisher again, Williams took ball one and then swung for the fences on the next pitch, but missed. Clearly he wanted to go out in style, and on the next pitch he delivered. Williams blasted the ball deep to right center. Center fielder Jackie Brandt watched it sail over his head, far past the wall, and crash on the canopy above the bench in the Red Sox bullpen, 440 feet away.

The emotional crowd showered their hero with adoration, yet Williams refused to break character, trotting around the bases with his head down as if it were just another at-bat. When he reached home plate, he shook hands with the next batter, rookie catcher Jim Pagliaroni, whose smile couldn't mask the tears in his eyes.

Williams chugged to the dugout and took a seat. For the next four minutes, teammates and fans — who chanted "We want Ted!" — urged him to take a curtain call. But that wasn't Williams' style. When he went to left field to start the ninth, the cheers roared like thunder. Manager Higgins sent Carroll Hardy to replace him before the top of the ninth started, and the deafening ovation continued as Ted trotted to the bench.

As Williams reached the dugout, it seemed he thought about tipping his cap, then decided not to. Instead, he descended the steps of the dugout . . . and there went the greatest hitter who ever lived.

Much more at home with a bat in his hand than a microphone in his face, Ted Williams shifts uncomfortably while addressing Red Sox fans before his final game, September 28, 1960, at Fenway Park. Williams played his entire career in Boston and came to love the fans.

CHAPTER 37

DOME, SWEET DOME

EIGHTH WONDER OF THE WORLD

April 12, 1965 — Houston: Walking into the first indoor baseball stadium ever built produced virtually the same reaction for players, officials and fans alike.

"Fantastic."

"Amazing."

"Indescribable."

"Unbelievable."

"What a stage."

every other park in the world will be antiquated."

A columnist for *The New York Times*, Arthur Daley, reported that "the only sight this wandering reporter ever saw that surpasses it is the exquisite Taj Mahal at Agra in India." He added, "Superlatives still can't do justice to the Astrodome, a fantasy that defies description."

The creation of Judge Roy Hofheinz, a former

The Houston Astrodome, which officially opened for business on April 9, 1965. The first indoor baseball park, it was immediately dubbed "The Eighth Wonder of the World."

One visiting Yankee player, here to help christen the Astrodome in an exhibition game, wondered if it was permissible to chew tobacco in what the local politicians called the Eighth Wonder of the World.

Longtime baseball executive Branch Rickey had perhaps the most profound comment upon seeing the new facility: "The day the doors on this park open,

mayor of Houston, the facility was officially known as the Harris County Domed Stadium when it was under construction but quickly changed its name to the Astrodome when the city franchise's name was changed from the Colt 45s to the Astros.

Hofheinz claimed he was inspired to develop the Astrodome after taking a tour of Rome, where he learned that the builders of the ancient Colosseum installed giant velariums to shield spectators from the Roman sun.

The subtropical weather in southern Texas made playing baseball difficult and uncomfortable because of the constant threat of rain, high humidity and a large infestation of mosquitoes. The concession stands at old Colt Stadium not only sold hot dogs and soda, but insect repellent as well. The team had just one sellout in its three seasons of playing at the stadium, for a doubleheader against the Dodgers.

The comfort of the fans would never be in doubt at the air-conditioned dome, where the temperature would be maintained at a constant 72 degrees. What turned out to be an unanticipated problem, however, quickly developed as the Astros played a series of exhibition games before taking on the Philadelphia

The indoor stadium also forced the Astros to come up with new ground rules never needed before. A batter would be out if a foul ball hit a speaker suspended from the ceiling and was caught by a fielder. However, a ball hitting the roof or a speaker in fair territory would be in play, officials said.

At its highest point, 208 feet above second base, an 18-story building could fit inside the building. The scoreboard alone measured six acres.

The weekend before the official opening game, The Astros played a series of exhibition games against the Yankees and Orioles. The honor of being the first hitter in the new stadium went to Mickey Mantle, when Yankees manager Johnny Keane purposely put him in the leadoff spot so "The Mick" would have that distinction.

Looking for the clubhouse, Mantle got lost in the

On April 10, 1965, the New York Yankees and Houston Astros played their second exhibition in the Astrodome. The park was used for Houston Astros baseball until the end of the 1999 season, when the team moved to a new downtown outdoor park.

Phillies in the first official game at the stadium.

The problem was that outfielders were unable to see fly balls because of the gridlike plastic dome, especially during day games. A research team from the DuPont Company met with the Astros to discuss possible solutions, including using orange baseballs, or giving the fielders various shades of sunglasses.

Team officials finally decided the best solution was to paint the ceiling – which had the effect of killing the natural grass on the field because it needed the sunlight to grow. The Astros were actually prepared to play on a completely dirt field until the Monsanto Company developed artificial grass for the facility, and gave it the appropriate name Astroturf.

cavernous stadium; for a while, he wasn't certain if he would actually make it to the plate. He had to stop at a concession stand and ask for directions.

When he finally did make it to the field, Mantle collected the first hit in the building's history, a single to center off Dick Farrell in the first inning. He later added the first home run, a 400-foot blast to center field.

President and Mrs. Lyndon Johnson were among the crowd of 47,876 at the game in the $31.6 million facility. The game had the atmosphere of a Broadway opening or a special theater production, from the well-dressed crowd to the upholstered, padded seats. Even the $1.50 pavilion seats, in place of bleachers, had seat cushions with rounded wooden backs. The Galaxie Gift Shop sold more than baseball caps and jerseys; one of store items was a $325 Lady Hamilton wristwatch. There also was a shoeshine stand located near the first level of seats.

The grounds crew, appropriately called Earthmen, wore uniforms consisting of orange space suits, black boots and white helmets.

For the first official game against the Phillies, 24 of America's 28 astronauts were on hand and each received a lifetime pass to all major-league games.

The Astros lost the game 2-0 on a two-run homer by Richie Allen in the third inning. Chris Short pitched a four-hit shutout for the Phillies, giving up two hits to Houston rookie second baseman Joe Morgan.

The unveiling of the new stadium came as the

In this April 9, 1965 photo, the Houston Astrodome — viewed through a fish-eye lens — looks more like a location shot for the movie *2001: A Space Odyssey*.

space race between the United States and the Soviet Union was escalating. In the stadium's inaugural year, two major developments occurred which spurred man's exploration of space. First, a Soviet cosmonaut became the first person to leave an orbiting spacecraft and float in outer space for 10 minutes. And in December, two Gemini spacecraft rendezvoused in space — a major step toward the planned manned flight to the moon.

In an era when Major League Baseball was trying to lure ever more fans with splashy, sometimes harebrained marketing schemes — Kansas City owner Charlie Finley hired a former Miss USA as a girl batboy — the Houston Astrodome proved to be the most spectacular, out-of-this-world attraction yet.

THE FAKE STUFF

Workmen at the Houston, Texas, Astrodome lay down sections of synthetic grass on June 21, 1966. The revolutionary plastic surface, called "Astroturf," of course needed no watering or cutting. As a result, it was used in half of the National League's ballparks by 1971.

Hitting a ball out of the stadium became impossible when the Astrodome opened in 1965, becoming the first enclosed stadium in major-league history.

Despite winning rave reviews and universal praise, there was not a mad rush by other franchises to follow the Astros' lead and build more domed stadiums. It was not until 1977 — 12 years later — that the next two enclosed stadiums opened: the Kingdome in Seattle and Olympic Stadium in Montreal.

What became much more popular with other teams was the creation of Astroturf, a synthetic grass that the Monsanto Company developed when natural grass died and could not be grown in the Astrodome. Until the Monsanto Company came to their rescue, it looked as if the Astros were going to be forced to play on an entire dirt field.

Once Astroturf was introduced, other teams quickly followed Houston's lead. While expensive to install, artificial grass turned out to be cheaper and easier to maintain than real grass in the long term. As the cookie-cutter stadiums opened, home to both baseball and football franchises, the fake grass became even more popular.

At one point in the 1970s, the Cardinals, Reds, Phillies, Pirates and Expos joined the Astros in playing on artificial grass. In the American League, Toronto, Minnesota, Seattle and Kansas City all installed artificial turf in their stadiums.

The only new stadiums that opened in the 1960s after the Astrodome that had natural grass fields were in Atlanta (Fulton County Stadium), Anaheim (Anaheim Stadium), Oakland (Oakland-Alameda County Stadium), St. Louis (Busch Memorial Stadium) and San Diego (San Diego Stadium).

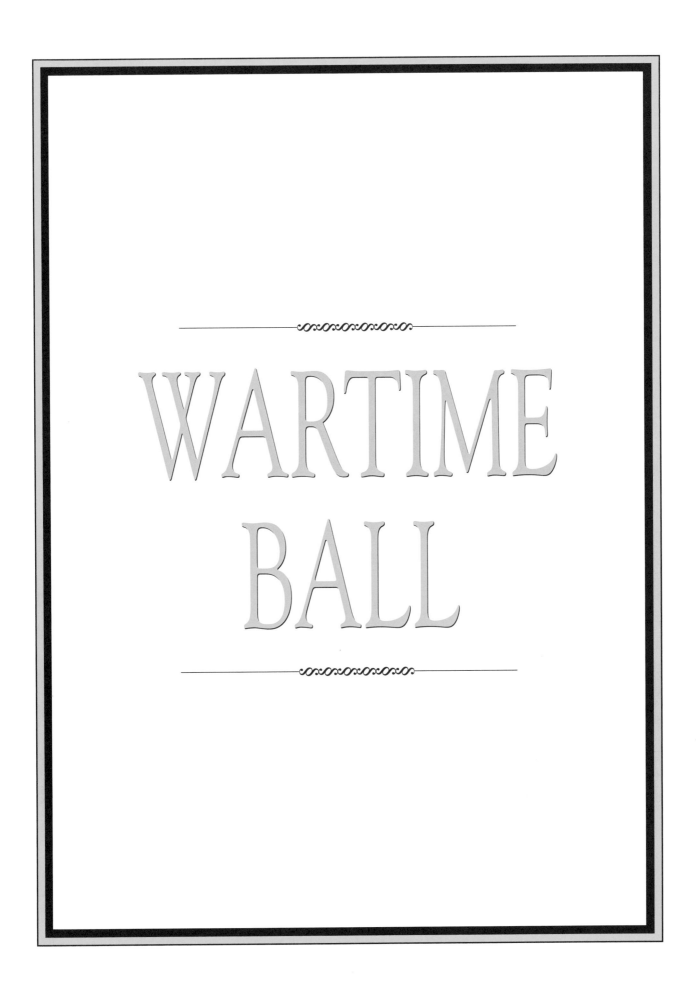

WARTIME
BALL

CHAPTER 38

THE STAR-CROSSED SERIES

HITTING AGAINST HITLER

For Hank Greenberg, it wasn't enough that Jews suffered discrimination across the world in the 1920s and 1930s. He was an outcast in his own Jewish community in the Bronx. His parents wanted their gangly teenager to go to college and become a doctor, lawyer, or teacher, but all Hank wanted to do was play the game he loved.

"Jewish women on my block . . . would point me out as a good-for-nothing, a loafer, and a bum

scoffed at Hank embraced him as a hero — the best Jewish baseball player anyone had ever seen. A handsome, regal slugger, Greenberg was the new Lou Gehrig. He drove in 170 runs in 1935 and an astounding 183 in 1937.

In 1938 Greenberg made a serious run at Babe Ruth's major-league record of 60 home runs. Though he was beloved by teammates and Tigers fans, some opponents and fans taunted him with

Left: Greenberg sits in the Tigers clubhouse at Briggs Stadium in May 1941, shortly before his induction into the U.S. Army. Right: Standing amid fellow inductees, Hank Greenberg (second from right), takes the oath of allegiance as soldier #36,114,611 in the U.S. Army. The ceremony took place on May 7, 1941, in Detroit Michigan.

who always wanted to play baseball rather than go to school," Greenberg recalled. "Friends and relatives sympathized with my mother because she was the parent of a big gawk who cared more for baseball . . . than school books. I was Mrs. Greenberg's disgrace."

By 1934, when he slugged 63 doubles and drove in 139 runs for the Detroit Tigers, those who had

bigoted slurs. During a heated contest against the White Sox in 1938, a Chicago player called him a "Jew son of a bitch." And over the last five games of the season, Hank was stuck on 58 home runs. Some fans believed that it wouldn't be right if a Jew broke the record of an American legend. Greenberg was walked frequently over the last few games, and he fell short of Ruth's fabled record.

As the 1930s wore down, Greenberg realized that other Jews faced far worse anti-Semitism. In Germany, Adolf Hitler and the Nazi Party had risen to power. On September 1, 1939, they invaded Poland and soon began transporting Jews to walled-off ghettos. Over the next six years, the Nazis and their collaborators would murder six million European Jews.

As a ballplayer, Greenberg could do little except disprove the Nazis' assertion that Jews were inferior human beings. "I came to feel that if I, as a Jew, hit a home run, I was hitting one against Hitler," he said.

In 1940 the Detroit draft board classified Greenberg as 4F (unfit for service) due to "flat feet." But Hank, amid unfounded rumors that he had bribed the board, asked to be reexamined, and he was found fit to serve. Greenberg was scheduled

Greenberg's first few months in the service were relatively uneventful, although one moment stood out. While playing an exhibition game against Michigan convicts, he blasted the ball out of the prison yard. "I'll get it! I'll get it!" the inmates joked.

Greenberg was discharged from the Army on December 5, 1941. Two days later, however, the Japanese attacked Pearl Harbor.

"We are in trouble," Greenberg told the Associated Press, "and there is only one thing to do — return to service." Hank immediately enlisted as an officer candidate in the Air Corps. After doing inspection work at air bases, he requested a transfer to a war zone. He was sent to the China-Burma-India Theater and flew on missions over the Himalayas. Eventually, he earned the rank of captain as well as four battle stars.

Hank Greenberg, center, explains to Army colleagues in February 1942 how he grips a bat. Greenberg was assigned to the Special Services section of the Army Air Forces.

to begin his tour of duty on May 7, 1941. The story was all over the media — in newspapers and on radio and newsreels — since Hank was the first baseball star of the era to enlist.

On May 6, Greenberg played the hero, belting two home runs against New York. Even the Yankees honored the sacrifice Hank was about to make for his country. In Greenberg's last at-bat of the game, Yankees catcher Bill Dickey told him that he would call only fastballs as a farewell gift. Although Hank swung and missed on three pitches, Dickey made good on his promise.

When his service finally ended in 1945, Greenberg returned to Detroit. For four years, he had dreamed of parking a fat pitch into the upper deck of Briggs Stadium. On July 1, a full house showered their returning idol with a standing ovation. As in his 1941 farewell game, he marked his comeback contest with a home run — a long blast in the eighth inning.

On the last day of the season, a doubleheader at St. Louis, Greenberg outdid himself. The Tigers needed to win one of the two games to clinch the pennant. Down 4-3 in the ninth to the Browns,

Hank belted a grand slam to send Detroit to the World Series.

He went deep twice in the fall classic against the Cubs before injuring his hand in Game 6. Unable to swing properly in Game 7, he moved runners along with a bunt in the first inning, contributing to a five-run rally. The Tigers prevailed, 9-3.

Over time, fans came to recognize Greenberg as a great man — not only as a baseball star and a war veteran, but as a compassionate human being. While other star athletes had been born with the proverbial silver spoon, Hank had experienced shame, bigotry, and the horrors of war. Humble and appreciative for what he had, he greeted fans

Detroit Tigers first baseman Hank Greenberg is shown in uniform at Fort Custer, Michigan, on May 8, 1941. Greenberg's term in the U.S. Army paid him the princely sum of $21 per month.

warmly, contributed to numerous causes, and reached out to the truly unfortunate.

Recalled Louis Blumberg, a friend of Greenberg: "There was a little crippled kid who sold pencils outside the Leland. Worst case of paralysis I ever saw. His face was all twisted — I never understood a word he said. But Hank was always doing things for that kid. He'd have him up for dinner in his suite or the dining room. It was as if he saw something in him, something that might have been if he hadn't had such a bad break in life."

THE GREATNESS OF GREENBERG

Dozens of players have exceeded Greenberg's 331 career home runs, yet the "Jewish Babe Ruth" reigns as one of the greatest sluggers of all time. "Greenberg," said longtime Tigers teammate Charlie Gehringer, "was our big gun. A strong guy. He had long arms and a big arc to his swing, so even if he was fooled on a pitch, he could still hit the ball a long ways."

Some of Greenberg's clouts remain part of baseball lore. On May 22, 1937, he crushed the longest ball that ever had been hit at Boston's Fenway Park. It sailed past the flagpole in center field and left the stadium. Over the next 12 months, Hank became the first hitter ever to reach the center field stands at Yankee Stadium and the first to belt one into the center field bleachers at Chicago's Comiskey Park

In 1938 Greenberg socked 58 home runs — second most ever at the time. Had he not missed 4 1/2 years to service during World War II, he very well could have topped 500 four-baggers — a milestone achieved prior to 1950 by only Babe Ruth, Jimmie Foxx, and Mel Ott. For his career, Hank averaged 0.92 RBI per game, a major-league record he shares with Lou Gehrig. He drove in 170 runs in 1935 and 183 in 1937. His .605 slugging percentage was the fifth best in the 20th century.

Greenberg damaged pitchers figuratively and literally. On May 25, 1935, he rifled a pitch off of Boston pitcher Fritz Ostermueller's face, breaking his cheekbone and several of his teeth. While Ostermueller writhed in pain on the way to the hospital, Greenberg unloaded on his replacement, crushing a home run in his next at-bat.

CHAPTER 39

THE BAMBINO VS. THE BIG TRAIN

ONE FOR THE BOYS

August 23, 1942 — New York: Eight long years had passed since Babe Ruth had satisfied his most primitive need: to dress in New York pinstripes and club a home run into Yankee Stadium's upper reaches. Now, at age 47 — overweight, graying and feeling the effects of a lifetime of unhealthy habits

help the dependents of those in the military. MLB did so by staging Army-Navy Games — big-league contests in which gate revenue would go to the cause. By August 1942, the most any team had raised in such a game was $57,000, but the Yankees attempted to top that with an extravaganza

Baseball Hall of Famer Babe Ruth warms up for photographers at New York's Yankee Stadium Aug. 21, 1942. The Babe was preparing for an exhibition against pitching great Walter Johnson to raise money for the Army-Navy Relief Fund during World War II.

— Ruth got another chance to swing for the seats. To sweeten the moment, his opponent on the hill would be 56-year-old Walter Johnson, universally regarded as the greatest pitcher who ever lived.

The duel between the two Hall of Famers was meant to support the war effort. After the United States entered World War II in December 1941, Major League Baseball offered to raise $500,000 to

planned for August 23.

Between games of the New York-Washington doubleheader, Yankees general manager Ed Barrow scheduled crowd-pleasing exhibitions. Members of the Yankees and Senators would square off in a 60-yard dash, as well as a relay race. Pitchers on each team, armed with fungo bats, would compete in a longball-hitting contest. Catchers would participate in a throwing-accuracy exhibition, firing from home plate to second base. But the main event — the matchup that would capture the public's imagination – would be the immortal Bambino versus Johnson, the legendary "Big Train."

More than 69,000 packed themselves into the "House That Ruth Built" to witness — and relive — history. From 1915 to 1927 (the year in which he cracked 60 home runs en route to the world title), Ruth had belted 10 home runs off the Senators ace. Johnson, who had recorded 417 wins in his career, spent his retirement on his farm in

Laughing, Ruth replied, "Hell, I'll be lucky to hit one at all. But I'll try to pull 'em down the line."

Johnson no longer possessed his blazing fastball, but he still threw with an easy motion. On the fifth pitch, Ruth lined the ball into lower right field stands. Later, on the 20th and last toss, the Babe launched a Ruthian blast — a towering drive down the right field line.

As Ruth began his familiar home run trot, the ball crash-landed in the third deck, detonating a thunderous roar from the crowd.

Baseball fans attending the Washington Senators/New York Yankees doubleheader at Yankee Stadium on August 23, 1942 got a thrill from a between-games exhibition put on by this great foursome. For the benefit of the Army-Navy relief fund, the following baseball luminaries took the field (left to right): former Washington mound great Walter Johnson; Benny Bengough, former catcher; Billy Evans, one of the greatest umpires ever to call a play; and Yankees slugger Babe Ruth.

Maryland. Ruth, still the most popular sports figure on the globe, was bedridden just a few days earlier by a bad cold.

Prior to their duel, Johnson said to Ruth, "Babe, I just want to ask one thing. Don't hit any back to me."

The ball actually curved foul, but no one seemed to care. As he circled the bases, the Babe tipped his cap to his ecstatic fans. For one glorious moment, it was 1927 all over again.

CHAPTER 40

ONE-ARMED WONDER

GRAY'S BRIEF HEYDAY

In the early decades of the 20th century, making a living in rural America wasn't easy — especially if you were the one-armed son of a coal miner. Such was the lot of Pete Wyshner, born on a winter day in Nanticoke, Pennsylvania, in 1915.

When Pete was a small boy (age six or seven, he recalled), a peddler offered him a quarter to help him sell apples and potatoes. At one point on that fateful date, Pete jumped off the man's truck. His right arm got caught in a churning wheel's spokes, and it was mangled so badly that doctors needed to amputate. A natural righty, Pete had to learn how to do everything left-handed.

Growing up, Pete became a remarkably good baseball player. Catching and running were the easy parts, yet he could hit as well. Standing in the left batter's box, he swatted a steady stream of line drives and could even put a charge into the ball. The hardest aspect of the game was throwing after the catch, but Pete — an outfielder — mastered this as well. "I'd catch the ball, stick the glove under my stump, roll the ball across my chest, and throw it back in," he explained. "No big deal."

Pete became so good, in fact, that he dreamed of playing professional ball. The idea of a one-armed pro ballplayer

Pete Gray, the St. Louis Browns' one-armed outfielder, shows his fielding form in this series of images from 1945. He wore his glove loosely on his fingertips and quickly tossed it to the ground, flipping the ball in the air and unleashing a throw toward the infield with his left hand.

seemed preposterous. But in the early 1930s — during the darkest days of the Great Depression — many preferred to pursue far-fetched dreams than to submit to bleak reality. Pete decided to go for it; he dropped out of high school and sought pro teams that would give him a shot.

For some reason, Pete thought he wouldn't get into the major leagues with a name like Wyshner, so he changed his last name to Gray. Pete Gray amazed fans with his all-around game. He hit for high averages, racked up doubles and even the occasional homer, and stole bases almost at will. Gray beat out drag bunts, virtually never struck out, and rarely erred in the outfield.

After playing semipro ball for the Bushwicks in Brooklyn, Gray got his first big break in 1938. A friend who owned a baseball school recommended him to Trois Rivieres of the Quebec Provincial League — but didn't mention Pete's handicap. When Gray arrived in Montreal, the team's manager met him at the train station. Pete had his coat draped over his stump, and when he took it off the manager was astonished.

"What's the matter with your right arm?" he asked.

"I don't have one."

"My God!"

Skeptical of the one-armed man, the manager first used him as a pinch hitter in a home game. The crowd hushed as Gray emerged from the dugout — but erupted when he cracked a base hit. Trois Rivieres won, and fans honored their new hero by showering him with currency.

With most of the stars off to war, big-league rosters were loaded with 4-F men (those physically unfit for duty) and older players. With the talent pool thin, some major-league clubs gave "novelty" players a chance. In 1944 the Cincinnati Reds allowed 15-year-old Joe Nuxhall to pitch in a game. In 1945 Bert Shepard, who had an artificial leg due to a war

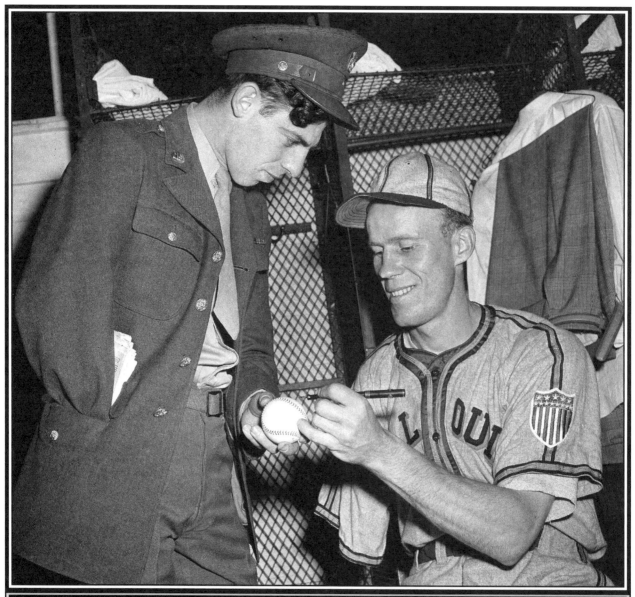

On April 26, 1945, Browns outfielder Pete Gray signs an autograph for U.S. soldier Pfc. Pat Gervace of Cleveland, who had lost his right arm in combat in December 1944.

Gray was an inspiration to thousands of men and women who persevered through physical problems.

As years passed, Gray moved on to more competitive leagues. In 1943 he signed with the Memphis Chicks, a Class-A team in the Southern Association. Though the Chicks were accused of exploiting Pete as a "freak attraction" to draw fans during the war, Gray proved he could play. He rapped .289, played errorless ball, and attracted national attention. The next season with Memphis, he swatted .333 and stole 68 bases, tying the league record. He was named the Southern Association's Most Valuable Player.

injury, fulfilled his big-league dream for the Washington Senators. But the most amazing story of all was Pete Gray.

Purchased by the St. Louis Browns for $20,000, Gray hit well for the American League club in spring training in 1945 and made the 25-man roster. On Opening Day, he cracked a hard single off Detroit ace Hal Newhouser, the reigning AL MVP. On May 20 against the New York Yankees, Gray ripped three hits and made a dazzling catch.

Browns manager Luke Sewell marveled at Gray's ability:

"He shows us something every day. You really don't believe some of the things he does. Believe me, he can show plenty of two-handed outfielders plenty."

For Gray, however, reality kicked in early in the season. He batted just .188 through April. His teammates, instead of praising him for his courage, resented his presence; some complained that he was only on the team as a gate attraction and that he was costing the Browns a pennant. A loner by nature, Gray felt even more isolated due to his subpar play and his teammates' hostility. One day, when he asked Browns pitcher Sig Jakucki for help tying his shoe, Jakucki shot back, "Tie your own [expletive] shoe, you [expletive]!"

As the season wore on, Gray spent more and more time on the bench. His final line in 1945: 77 games, a .218 batting average, six doubles, two triples, and five steals in 11 attempts. He struck out only 11 times in 234 at-bats, and he made seven errors. The Browns finished six games out of first place.

Pete Gray shows his one-armed batting style during St. Louis Browns spring training, March 23, 1945.

Gray knew that 1945 would be his one and only season in the major leagues. With the war ending, all the legitimate big-leaguers would be back in 1946. He took his fate in stride. After all, he said, "all I wanted to do was to play one game in the big leagues."

Eventually, Gray returned to a quiet life in his hometown of Nanticoke. He avoided reporters, but he liked to give advice to the young people of his community — be it tips about baseball or encouraging words about overcoming adversity. Recalled a neighbor: "He was a very nice and gentle person who would share a good baseball story with you, one who was willing to sit and talk for hours on end about everything . . . He would have this certain glow about him whenever he talked about his memories."

Gray died in June 2002, just five days before the death of Ted Williams. Astute reporters noted that in the same week baseball mourned the loss of the best able-bodied hitter — and the greatest one-armed batter — who had ever lived. It was a deserving epitaph for a coal miner's son who had dared to dream big.

THE ONE-LEGGED PITCHER

Bert Shepard (left), who had lost part of his right leg in World War II, adjusts his artificial limb on March 30, 1945. Shepard was in camp trying out for the Washington Senators, and actually pitched one game for the big club later that season. Senators manager Ossie Bluege looks on.

Pete Gray wasn't the only physically challenged player to play big-league ball during the war years. Bert Shepard, who got his foot shot off during World War II, subsequently became the only one-legged player in MLB history.

As an Indiana farm boy in 1937, Shepard hopped on a freight train and headed to California, figuring that was the place to be if you wanted to become a professional baseball player. He worked odd jobs and eventually hooked on as a minor-league pitcher. War intervened, however, and in 1942 the U.S. Army drafted Shepard.

Shepard excelled as a fighter pilot, but after dozens of missions he was shot down in Germany in May 1944. He awoke in a German hospital several days later, his left leg amputated. Liberated from Stalag IX-C in October 1944, Shepard walked with a wooden limb and continued to try to pitch. The Washington Senators were so impressed with his moxie that they signed him to a contract in 1945.

On August 4, 1945, two days before the United States bombed Hiroshima, the Senators were getting blown out by the Boston Red Sox. With the bases loaded and two outs in the fourth inning, Shepard was called in to face Catfish Metkovich. "I was awful glad about it," Shepard recalled. "I said, 'Goddamn it, I'm in the ballgame!'"

With the count full, the southpaw struck out Metkovich with the bases loaded, earning a standing ovation from the Senators crowd. Shepard proceeded to hold Boston to one run in 5 1/3 innings. Though he would never pitch in the majors again, Bert Shepard remains a big-league legend.

WHEN THE
RECORDS
FELL

CHAPTER 41

DOUBLE NO-NOS

VANDER MEER'S BIG NIGHT

June 15, 1938 — Brooklyn: It was a night like none other in Brooklyn. Olympic sprint champion Jesse Owens out legged several players in exhibition races and broad jumped 23 feet. A band played, as did a fife and drum corps, entertaining some 40,000 fans. Another 15,000 were turned away at the gate, which was closed 45 minutes early, to avoid a fire code violation.

Dodgers president Lee McPhail leaned back in

Vander Meer actually warmed up three times. The huge crowd and pregame festivities had caused the game's first pitch to be delayed. Among those in the seats was a contingent of about 500 from Vander Meer's hometown of Midland, New Jersey. They had organized a bus trip to the game and presented their native son with a gold watch in a pregame ceremony to commemorate his first no-hitter. Vander Meer's parents, sister and girlfriend were also at the game.

Johnny Vander Meer of the Cincinnati Reds pitches to Buddy Hassett of the Brooklyn Dodgers in the fifth inning at Brooklyn's Ebbets Field on June 15, 1938. In this game, the first major-league night game played in the East, Vander Meer pitched his second consecutive no-hitter.

his seat and soaked up the atmosphere. The occasion? The first night baseball game at Ebbets Field, and McPhail had pulled out all the stops. The great Babe Ruth highlighted a gathering of celebrities. He waved to the adoring crowd and then shook hands with Cincinnati pitcher Johnny Vander Meer, congratulating the 23-year-old on throwing a no-hitter against Boston four days earlier.

But as it turned out, it was not the debut of night baseball that would make this game one for the history books. Two hours and 22 minutes after the opening pitch, the Ebbets Field crowd would instead be celebrating Vander Meer's unprecedented second consecutive no-hitter – a feat wholly befitting the pomp and ceremony preceding its attainment.

Vander Meer, a left-hander with great movement

on his fastball and a sharp-breaking curve, was in just his second major-league season. He had tried out for both Boston and Brooklyn earlier in his career but had failed to stick, which made his accomplishment for Cincinnati that much more rewarding. Not that Johnny was looking for a no-hitter in either case. Any win was a good win for a pitcher who never tallied more than 18 victories in a season and finished his career with a losing record (119-121).

Vander Meer had spent most of the previous summer in the minor leagues. What time he did spend in Cincinnati was not very impressive. He walked 69 men against 52 strikeouts and lost two more games than he won (3-5). Manager Bill McKechnie saw talent in the young southpaw, however, and spent considerable time in the spring of 1938 altering Vander Meer's delivery and improving

base by strong-armed catcher Ernie Lombardi. Those three free passes were all Vander Meer would yield. He struck out four and did not allow a man to reach second base in a 3-0 gem.

One Vander Meer no-hitter was cause enough for jubilation. It was the first by a Reds pitcher since Hod Eller in 1919; and it made a strong case for Johnny to be on the mound when the All-Star Game came to Cincinnati's Crosley Field in July. The task at hand, however, was the first game under the lights in the Big Apple — a tall order for a youngster coming off the best performance of his life.

Control was a bigger problem for Vander Meer in Brooklyn. He walked eight batters, but inning after inning, the Dodgers went down without a hit. By the time two Brooklyn batters drew walks in the seventh, the Dodgers might as well have been the visiting team. Cincinnati had scored four runs in the third

Overpowering left-handed hurler Johnny Vander Meer won 15 games as a rookie in 1938, including his two no-hitters, and 119 in his big-league career.

his control. Vander Meer entered the June 11 game against the visiting Boston Bees holding the National League lead with 52 strikeouts and a 5-2 ledger.

Ten days after Action Comics put the first Superman issue on the shelves, Vander Meer did his own superhero impersonation. He retired the first nine men in order and used a double play in the fourth inning, after yielding a walk, to make it 12 up and 12 down. He walked two more batters in the fifth but one was caught taking too big a lead at first

and was in no danger of losing. The capacity crowd knew it might be witnessing history, and cheered wildly when the visiting Vander Meer worked out of the jam.

It was 6-0 by the bottom of the ninth inning, and the only drama remaining was Vander Meer's historic quest. Buddy Hassett hit a weak grounder down the first base line. Vander Meer picked it up and tagged Hassett himself. One out. The pressure mounted, and it appeared to be getting to the Reds pitcher.

He walked Babe Phelps, Cookie Lavagetto and Dolf Camilli consecutively, loading the bases. McKechnie did not walk to the mound; he ran. "Take it easy, Johnny," he reportedly told his pitcher, "but get the no-hitter." Mentioning a no-hitter in progress, of course, has long been a baseball faux pas.

Watching from the bleachers, Vander Meer's 15-year-old sister Garberdina was more concerned about her brother's history of control problems than any jinx. "That was scary," she said of the ninth-inning walks. "I thought maybe he would lose it then."

Vander Meer had been throwing smoke earlier in the game. Now, he was relying heavily on his curveball. McKechnie's talk seemed to calm his nerves. He coaxed a grounder to third base from Ernie Koy. Lew Riggs threw home for the force out,

Johnny Vander Meer signs autographs for enraptured kids from his hometown of Highland Park, New Jersey, which he visited the day after his second no-hitter.

bringing Leo Durocher to the plate with two down.

After a questionable "ball" call from home plate umpire Bill Stewart on what looked like a sure third strike, Durocher lofted a 2-2 pitch into short center.

"Boy, did Harry Craft squeeze that ball," teammate Lonny Frey said. "That ballpark was bedlam after the last out."

Fans rushed from the seats. His teammates hoisted Vander Meer onto their shoulders, not so much in celebration of his accomplishment, but to keep fans from ripping his jersey to shreds.

Hours later, however, all was peaceful in Vander Meer's world. While a band of reporters waited at his family's New Jersey home — the *Cincinnati Post*'s headline the next day called the double no-hitter the greatest feat in baseball history — Vander Meer temporarily eluded the limelight by keeping a fishing date with a friend.

A THIRD NO-HITTER?

No stranger to firsts, Vander Meer warms up at the first night game at Ebbets Field, June 15, 1938.

How do you top consecutive no-hitters in your first full major-league season? Truly, you don't. However, Vander Meer was not content with one milestone feat and a fishing trip. He continued his assault on the record books even after his unprecedented pitching achievement in 1938.

In his next outing, June 19 at Boston, Johnny pitched no-hit baseball into the fourth inning. Debs Garms then singled to left center field, ending Vander Meer's record hitless streak at 21 2/3 innings — including the final out from his start prior to the first no-hitter. That mark, too, appears to be in little danger of falling any time soon.

It was a breakthrough season for Vander Meer, who went 15-10 and was named Major League Pitcher of the Year. It was the first of six seasons in which he won 10 or more games. In 1943 he tied his idol Carl Hubbell's record by striking out six batters in the All-Star Game.

The high times were temporary, though. A tour in the U.S. Navy in 1944 and 1945 and arm trouble cut Vander Meer's career short. When he retired one game into the 1951 season, Vander Meer's record was a modest 119 wins against 121 losses. Wherever he went thereafter, stories and questions about his well-known accomplishment followed.

"Kids are always chasing rainbows," Vander Meer once said. "Baseball is a world where they can catch them."

CHAPTER 42

HERE'S TO YOU, JOE DIMAGGIO

JOLTIN' JOE'S HITTING STREAK

July 17, 1941 — Cleveland: As Joe DiMaggio's record-breaking hitting streak surpassed the two-month mark, even people who didn't follow baseball got caught up in the frenzy, wondering how long he could keep it going.

The expanding war in Europe between Nazi Germany and Russia dominated the national headlines, as did reports of escalating tensions between the United States and Japan. These grim news stories

additional writers were covering DiMaggio's exploits.

The national attention had begun to build as DiMaggio's streak increased. The streak started on May 15, against the White Sox at Yankee Stadium, and as it climbed past 20 games, then 30 games, the media and baseball fans took notice. As DiMaggio and the Yankees came into other towns, the home-standing team often took out a full-page advertisement saluting DiMaggio's streak and

New York Yankees outfielder Joe DiMaggio singles in the first inning against the Cleveland Indians at Cleveland, July 16, 1941. It was the 56th straight game in which he got a hit. The following night, his record-breaking streak ended with an 0-for-4 performance.

provided even more reason to turn quickly to the sports page for a diversion. DiMaggio's streak immediately became the hot story.

Radio stations interrupted whatever program was on the air when the bulletins crossed the wire about DiMaggio getting another hit. The Yankees had to add an extra car to their private train because so many

encouraging fans to come out to the games.

The modern-day record for most consecutive games with at least one hit had been 41, set by George Sisler of the St. Louis Browns in 1922. On June 29, in the first game of a doubleheader at Washington, DiMaggio tied that mark.

Like any good news story, DiMaggio's streak had

its share of shadowy intrigue. Between games in the Washington doubleheader, DiMaggio's favorite bat was stolen out of the bat rack in the dugout; as a result, he had to use a different bat in the second game. It looked as if the streak might end at that point when DiMaggio began the game 0-for-3. But in the seventh inning, he finally came through with a single to left in his fourth at-bat.

DiMaggio's next target was Wee Willie Keeler, who had set his mark of hitting in 44 consecutive

catch smashes by DiMaggio and throw him out at first both times. In the eighth, facing Bagby with the bases loaded, DiMaggio grounded to short to start a doubleplay.

It looked as if the Indians might rally to tie the game in the ninth and perhaps send it into extra innings, giving DiMaggio another chance to extend the streak. They had the tying run on third with nobody out, but failed to score.

"That play Ken Keltner made on me in the first

Joe DiMaggio, right, of the New York Yankees, congratulates Boston Red Sox slugger Ted Williams, whose ninth-inning homer defeated the National League All Stars, 7-5, in Detroit, July 8, 1941. It was quite a season for both men. DiMaggio hit in 56 straight games en route to a .357 average, while Williams batted .406, becoming the last man to clear the .400 barrier.

games before the turn of the century. That record fell with a fifth-inning home run on July 2 — an accomplishment that prompted all of the writers in the press box to stand and join the fans in applauding DiMaggio as he circled the bases.

The streak continued past 50 games, and reached 56 when DiMaggio had three hits against the Indians on July 16. Stories were already being written that this might be the sports record that would never be broken.

On July 17, before 67,468 fans at Municipal Stadium, the largest crowd ever to see a night game, Indians pitchers Al Smith and Jim Bagby combined to keep DiMaggio hitless in three at-bats, although he did draw one walk. The streak was over.

Twice DiMaggio was robbed by Indians third baseman Ken Keltner, who went behind the base to

inning, when he went behind third for a backhand stop of that hard smash was a beautiful piece of work," DiMaggio said. "When they take 'em away from you like that there's nothing a fellow can do about it."

Many thought DiMaggio would be relieved to see his streak come to an end, since the omnipresent reporters' attention would now be diverted elsewhere. But DiMaggio actually felt otherwise.

"I can't say that I'm glad it's over," DiMaggio said. "Of course I wanted to go on as long as I could. Now that the streak is over, I just want to get out there and keep helping to win ball games."

Perhaps because he had already received national attention for setting a Pacific Coast League record by hitting in 61 consecutive games, DiMaggio seemed comfortable in the glare of media attention.

He routinely gave interviews to newspaper

reporters covering the streak, including a lengthy chat with *The New York Times*. On the day he extended the streak to 56 games, DiMaggio spoke with reporters from Cleveland's newspaper, *The Plain Dealer*.

Long features and profiles of DiMaggio appeared in all of the leading national magazines as well, including *Life*, *Look*, *Collier's*, and *The Saturday Evening Post*.

DiMaggio even seemed unimpressed that bandleader Les Brown and his Band of Renown

record — trying to finish the season with a .400 batting average. During his streak, DiMaggio hit .408 with 15 home runs.

DiMaggio, who had added another unofficial game to his streak by getting a hit in the All-Star game, fell five games short of tying his own personal record hitting streak of 61 games in a row. He had set that record when he was an 18-year-old in 1933, playing with his hometown San Francisco Seals in the Pacific Coast League.

Even in retirement, DiMaggio had that smooth swing. Here, he connects for a double off Lefty Grove in the annual Old-Timers' Game at Yankee Stadium in New York, July 30, 1955. Former Chicago Cubs standout Gabby Hartnett is the catcher for the Hall of Fame team, which faced a squad composed of ex-Yankees stars. The Yankees Old Timers won 7-3.

thought the streak worthy of a song. "Joltin' Joe DiMaggio" was released as the streak was nearing its zenith. Written by New York disc jockey Alan Courtney and Ben Homer, "Joltin' Joe DiMaggio" became a big hit across the country.

DiMaggio's streak came as he was battling for attention with another young baseball star, Ted Williams, who had his sights set on another baseball

At that time, nobody knew how to spell his name correctly. Even the *San Francisco Chronicle* repeatedly referred to him as de Maggio in headlines and stories about the streak.

Eight years later, every fan in the country, and even around the world, knew DiMaggio's name and could spell it correctly.

CHAPTER 43

RAPID ROBERT

FELLER'S FURIOUS FASTBALL

Teams couldn't spend much on scouting in the mid-1930s, but around that time, the Cleveland Indians caught wind of an Iowa high school pitcher with a roaring fastball. Bob Feller, who had grown strong while performing chores on his father's farm, fired five no-hitters for Van Meter High. Violating a Major League Baseball rule that prohibited the signing of players without a high school diploma, Cleveland inked the young phenom to a contract. Though fined $7,500 for their misdeed, the Indians were allowed to keep their prize recruit.

Immediately, "Rapid Robert" was hailed as the second coming of Walter Johnson. As he wound up, Feller pivoted backward, then turned and rocketed his fastball toward the plate. "I just reared back and let them go," he said. He also packed a big-breaking curveball that was more like an optical illusion.

In his debut with the Indians in July 1936, the 17-year-old Feller struck out eight St. Louis Cardinals in three innings during an exhibition game. In his first official major league start in August, he fanned 15 St. Louis Browns. In a September game, he whiffed 17 Philadelphia A's, tying the major-league record. He then went back to Van Meter to finish high school.

From 1937 through 1941, Feller's fastball was all the rage. "If anybody threw that ball any harder than Rapid Robert," said fellow speedballer Satchel Paige, "then the human eye couldn't follow it." Feller struck out 150 batters in 149 innings in 1937. He then led the American League with 240 in 1938 — including an MLB-record 18 on the last day of the season. Over the next three seasons, the perennial All-Star won 76 games and tossed an Opening Day no-hitter in 1940.

During World War II, Feller missed four seasons while serving in the United States Navy, where he earned eight battle stars. When he returned to the Indians in 1946, he was better than ever, thanks to a new slider. He no-hit the Yankees on April 30 and finished the season with 26 wins and 348 strikeouts, one shy of Rube Waddell's big-league record.

In the pre-radar gun era, people used various machines to gauge Feller's fastball. On August 20, 1946, U.S. Army personnel employed a sophisticated device — a Sky Screen Chronograph — to register the speed of Feller's fastball. He checked in at a feverish 98.6 mph, breaking the record of 94.7 mph that the Yankees' Atley Donald had recorded in 1939. At the Aberdeen Proving Grounds, a speeding motor cycle test also clocked Feller's heater at 98.6 mph. Feller was also clocked at 107.9 mph in a 1946 demonstration at Washington's Griffith Stadium; and he supposedly hit 104 mph on a speed-measurement device in Chicago.

No one will ever know exactly how hard Feller threw, but almost all of those who faced him said he was the fastest of his era. Mused Ted Lyons of the White Sox: "It wasn't until you hit against him that you knew how fast he really was, until you saw with your own eyes that ball jumping at you."

Enshrined in the Baseball Hall of Fame, Feller finished his major-league career with 266 victories in 1956.

Bob Feller, Cleveland Indians hurler, throws a ball (shown in the middle of the shot) through a U.S. Army chronograph at Griffith Stadium, Washington, D.C., August 20, 1946. Later in this session, one of his fastballs was timed at 145 feet per second, or 98.6 miles per hour. According to the Army, this shattered the previous mark of 139 feet per second registered by Atley "Swampy" Donald of the New York Yankees in 1939. Feller was universally known as the hardest thrower of his time and one of the fastest in baseball history.

Opposite: Bob Feller is shown here at age 19. Hailing from Van Meter, Iowa, Feller was already famous even before reaching the major leagues. His high leg kick helped him reach heretofore unknown fastball speeds, and he soon mastered his control enough to become a great major-league pitcher.

CHAPTER 44

MR. MACK

A'S MANAGER RETIRES AT 88

October 18, 1950 — Philadelphia: As America entered a new era after World War II, young baseball fans asked their folks about the tall, gray-haired gentleman in the Philadelphia A's dugout. Was he really the manager? Did he always wear a suit? And how old was he?

Parents informed their children that this was Mr. Connie Mack, known as the "grand old gentleman of the game." Mack had managed and co-owned the Philadelphia A's since 1901. He would hold both positions until retiring at the age of 88 on October 18, 1950.

While other managers wore baggy uniforms, cussed, and spat tobacco, Mack dressed like an East Coast politician (complete with his trademark straw hat) and appeared noble and virtuous. He rarely raised his voice and virtually never swore. He was kind to strangers and fair to his players. Even during 100-loss seasons, he delighted in the sights, sounds, and people at the ballpark. This is how postwar adults knew Connie Mack. However, few were aware of his rough-hewn behavior as a ballplayer, way back in the 1800s.

When Mack broke into professional baseball in 1886, the sport was very much a manly pursuit. The catcher donned just a pancake glove, a chest protector, and a primitive mask — no shin guards. Through 1892, pitchers fired their fastballs from just 50 feet away. Few catchers could endure more than a few dozen games a year behind the plate, but Mack — despite his tall, rail-thin frame — caught more games than most catchers. He was so tough, he deliberately smacked batters' bats with his glove while they took a rip. Since any caught foul tip was an out, even on the first pitch, Mack — on missed swings — sometimes mouthed the sound of a foul tip to trick the umpire into calling an out.

Mack managed the Pittsburgh Pirates in the mid-1890s. Because his team excelled in low-scoring contests, he froze the baseballs in an icebox before games. Other than that, the "Tall Tactician" was and remained an upstanding manager. In 1901, the inaugural year of the American League, he took charge of the Philadelphia Athletics — the A's — a team that he himself named.

Over the next 50 years, the A's were either dynastically good or embarrassingly awful. They won four pennants and three World Series from 1910 through 1914 — and then finished in the cellar for eight straight years. His 1929-31 A's ranked among the greatest teams ever, with such Hall of Famers as Jimmie Foxx, Al Simmons, Mickey Cochrane, and Lefty Grove. Mack eventually became sole owner of the A's. When attendance was down, however, he didn't have the financial resources to pay competitive salaries. As a result, from 1935 to 1950, the team finished in the basement 10 times.

Mack concluded his career with an all-time record 3,582 managerial wins. Yet as he famously said, "You can't win them all," and he didn't. His 3,841 losses are a record that will never be approached. It may be impossible to sum up a 67-year baseball career in two sentences, but famed Red Smith gave it a shot. "Connie entered the game when it was a game for roughnecks," Smith wrote. "He saw it become respectable, he lived to be a symbol of its integrity, and he enjoyed every minute of it."

On the eve of his 80th birthday when this photo was snapped, Mack still had job security. After all, he owned the team!

CHAPTER 45

61 IN '61

MARIS' LONELY QUEST

October 1, 1961 — New York: Two dramas were played out on this warm, fall afternoon at Yankee Stadium, the scene of many of baseball's most historic moments over the years.

While the nation watched to see if the Yankees' Roger Maris could become the first player in history to hit 61 home runs in a season, a battle raged among fans in the right field bleachers to be the one who caught the historic homer — and the money that went with it. Sam Gordon, a restaurant owner from Sacramento, California, promised to pay $5,000 to the lucky fan who caught the home run ball.

Maris, aware of the offer, had some advice for whoever might catch the home run — if he was lucky enough to hit it.

Maris follows through on his swing as he clubs his record-breaking 61st home run. Maris was voted the AL MVP in 1961 after also having won the award in 1960.

"If you catch it, don't give it to me," Maris said. "Take the $5,000."

Perhaps Maris was trying to be generous to the lucky fan. But for him, that home run ball symbolized more than just a record. It also represented all the hardships he had endured during the season while attempting to surpass the 60-homer barrier set by Babe Ruth in 1927.

The quiet and shy son of a North Dakota coal miner, Maris had signed a baseball contract instead of accepting a scholarship to play football for Bud Wilkinson at Oklahoma. Yet despite his impressive skills, Maris was not the golden boy of either the Yankees or their fans. If anybody was supposed to break the Babe's record, it was Mickey Mantle, the heir to the Yankee crown that had been passed down from Ruth to Joe DiMaggio to Mantle. Many fans believed that Maris, who had played in Cleveland and Kansas City before being traded to the Yankees prior to the 1960 season, was not worthy of wearing that crown.

Fan antipathy aside, Maris also had to contend with a ruling from Major League Baseball Commissioner Ford Frick. When both Maris and Mantle went on a home run surge early in the season, Frick had issued a ruling that raised the bar for sluggers attempting to smash Ruth's record. According to Frick's ruling, a player would have to hit more than 60 home runs in the first 154 games of the season, which was the length of the season in 1927. A player who hit that mark after that point in the season would have the record for a 162-game season, Frick said.

The American League had expanded by two teams in 1961, adding the Los Angeles Angels and the Washington Senators to the league, and had increased the length of the season by eight games. At the time of Frick's ruling, both Maris and Mantle were on a pace to break the record in the shorter time span; both said they agreed with Frick's decision. Nothing was said publicly about Frick having served as a ghostwriter for Ruth many years earlier.

Many reporters tried to imply that the race was a personal battle between Mantle and Maris, when that could not have been further from the truth. They were close friends, and even shared an apartment in Queens during the season with

Pappas in the third inning. Yet when he went hitless in his final three at-bats, the nation seemed to turn its attention away, believing Maris had failed to break the record.

Maris, however, did not consider himself a failure. After all of the abuse and criticism he had received from the media and fans, he still had a goal of hitting 61 or more home runs. It would be a personal record, rather than a major-league one.

Unfortunately, a physically and mentally exhausted Maris failed to homer in his next three games. On September 26, at home against the Orioles in the 158th game of the season, Maris

Yankees slugger Roger Maris leaves the batter's box after hitting his record-breaking 61st home run at Yankee Stadium on October 1, 1961, the last day of the season.

Maris broke Babe Ruth's single-season home run record in the fourth inning on a pitch from Tracy Stallard of the Boston Red Sox.

teammate Bob Cerv. Maris was being pressured from every other corner of his world, but not from Mantle.

He and his family received death threats. His hair began to fall out in clumps from the tension. Only on the field was he at peace, away from the reporters and photographers.

A virus knocked Mantle out of the race after he had hit his 53rd homer on September 10, but Maris kept charging and went into the 154th game of the season, against the Orioles in Baltimore, with 58 homers. With ABC-TV broadcasting the game, Maris became only the second player in history to hit 59 homers, with a blast off Milt

bounced back to score his 60th homer off Orioles pitcher Jack Fisher.

Coincidentally, one of the 19,000 fans in attendance that day was Ruth's widow Claire, who saw Maris' homer land only about 40 feet to the spot where her husband's 60th homer had landed 34 years earlier.

Four games remained in the season, but Maris sat out the next day. When he failed to homer against the Red Sox the next two games, the season, and his bid for major-league immortality, was down to one game.

A crowd of only 23,154 showed up at the Stadium, most paying either 75 cents for a seat in the right field bleachers or $3.50 for a box seat. The seats in left field were virtually empty.

In the fourth inning, Maris hit a 2-0 pitch from Boston rookie Tracy Stallard into the seats for home run number 61. One young fan jumped out of the stands and raced up to Maris as he rounded third base, shaking his hand. His teammates forced Maris to make four bows to the crowd before finally letting him into the dugout.

The lucky fan holding the prize baseball was Sal Durante, a 19-year-old truck driver from Brooklyn. Stadium police whisked him away before other fans could try to steal the ball.

Durante later met Maris and attempted to give him the ball, but he refused to take it. Gordon presented Durante with a check on the CBS-TV show *Calendar* and later turned the ball over to Maris.

"Whether I beat Ruth's record or not is for others to say," Maris said in the frenzied clubhouse.

Roger Maris and Sal Durante, 19, hold Maris' 61st home run ball in the runway at New York's Yankee Stadium, Oct. 1, 1961. Durante caught Maris' record-breaking home run in the right field stands.

"But it gives me a wonderful feeling to know that I'm the only man in history to hit 61 home runs. Nobody can take that away from me."

Stallard, now forever a part of history, felt the same way.

"I have nothing to be ashamed of," he said. "He hit sixty others, didn't he?"

The accomplishment did not change the popular perception of Maris. On the day following his record-setting home run, a column in *The New York Times* was entitled, "Angry King of Swat."

"Even the Yankee clubhouse attendants think I'm tough to live with," Maris said. "I guess they're right. I'm miffed most of the time regardless of how I'm doing. But regardless of my faults, I'll never take abuse from anybody — big or small, important or unimportant — if I think it's undeserved."

THE UNAPPRECIATED ROGER MARIS

Baseball might have never seen a more reluctant celebrity than Roger Maris.

He was happy and comfortable playing in virtual anonymity in Kansas City when he was traded to the Yankees in December 1959. He was not happy about the trade, and his family continued to live in Kansas City, despite his move to New York. Even though he was elected the American League MVP in 1960, nobody — including Maris — was prepared for what was about to happen to him in 1961.

In his first three seasons in the majors, with the Indians and Kansas City from 1957 to 1959, Maris had hit a combined total of 58 home runs. Even when he hit 39 in his 1960 season with the Yankees, there was no prediction or even thought that he was capable of hitting many more home runs than that total.

Because he was so unprepared for the pressure his assault on Babe Ruth's single-season home run record would produce, the 1961 season brought Maris more despair than happiness. Even after his historic season, Maris never received the praise and recognition such an accomplishment deserved.

For the final years of his career, Maris was always questioned about 1961. His highest home run total following that season before he retired in 1968 was 33. People viewed his 1961 season as an anomaly, and almost criticized Maris for it.

When he suffered a broken hand in May 1965, Maris was never told the hand was broken and was urged to work out to get back in the lineup. He would only learn that he'd broken his hand in September.

In 1966, Maris informed Yankees manager Ralph Houk that he planned to retire after the season. Houk talked him into delaying the announcement until the next spring, when the Yankees would allow him to retire as he wished. Instead, in December 1966 he was traded to the Cardinals.

Maris helped the Cardinals win the 1967 World Series. Cardinals team owner August A. Busch, Jr., persuaded Maris to play another year by promising him a beer distributorship. Maris finally did retire after the 1968 season, but his years out of baseball were not much happier than his final seasons in the game. He died of cancer at the age of 51 in 1985.

CHAPTER 46

RUNNING WILD

THE BASE THIEF

October 3, 1962 — Los Angeles: Just one year after Roger Maris rewrote baseball's record book by hitting 61 home runs, Maury Wills came running and sliding after him — either feet first or with a belly flop.

Wills stole the final three bases of his historic season in the third and deciding playoff game for the Dodgers against the Giants at Dodger Stadium. With these last three stolen bases, Wills brought his season total to a whopping 104 — breaking Ty Cobb's mark of 96 steals in a season that had stood since 1915.

breaking Cobb's record nor stealing 100 bases in a year had been goals he'd set for himself. All he wanted to do was play every game and hit .300.

"The thought never even occurred to me," Wills said. "I still don't see how I did it. I don't think it will ever be done again. Even after I had stolen 70 bases I never dreamed of the record, but they kept piling up."

It was not too long ago that even the thought of Wills playing regularly in the major leagues would have seemed a stretch. One of 12 children born to a Baptist minister in Washington, DC,

Maury Wills steals his 100th base of the 1962 season on September 27 against the Houston Colts. By this time, Wills was in nearly constant pain from sliding bruises on his legs.

Even though Wills had led the NL in stolen bases the previous two years, nobody could have predicted an assault on Cobb's record during the 1962 season. Wills' 50 steals in 1960 had been the most by a NL player since 1923; and nobody in the American League had stolen more than 61 bases since 1920.

Even Wills himself admitted that neither

Wills got his first chance to play professional baseball with the Giants, who gave him a tryout as a pitcher. Although Wills struck out nine batters in three innings, the Giants passed on signing him.

Wills signed with the Dodgers as an 18-year-old in 1951, but he languished in their minor leagues. After the 1958 season, he was conditionally sold to the Tigers for $35,000. Once they took a look at the next spring training, however, the Tigers sent him back to the Dodgers.

Adding further insult to injury, Topps Company, Inc. — the makers of baseball trading cards and Bazooka Bubble Gum — also passed on Wills. Both the Topps scout and the Dodgers' scouts advised the company not to sign Wills, who became the first player Topps ever passed on to make it to the majors. Since then, the company has signed contracts with every player, just in case.

During his ninth year in the minors, Wills became a switch-hitter at Spokane in 1959, thanks to Bobby Bragan. He was hitting .313 with 25 stolen bases when the Dodgers called him up in the middle of the season. He hit .260, and then joined the Dodgers as their regular shortstop the following year.

Just reaching the major leagues did not make Wills a success, however. He was thrown out trying to steal on his first three attempts for the Dodgers. But as he began studying the pitchers, looking for

frame of mind. I ran every time with the thought that the pitcher would make a perfect pitch and the catcher would make a perfect throw, and I'd still beat them. I never have a doubt."

Wills' assault on the record book began slowly, as he stole only eight bases in April. He stole 19 in May and 15 in June. He passed the 50 mark on July 27, in the Dodgers' 104th game, and people began to notice. Twenty-two steals in August boosted his total to 73, just seven away from the NL record of 80 set by Bob Bescher of the Reds in 1911.

All of the steals took a physical toll on Wills, and a mental toll on his opponents. Late in the year he began to resort to belly-slides so he could try to protect his legs. His hips were so bruised he could not stand the pain.

On September 7, he stole four bases against Pittsburgh, tying and passing Bescher's record. When Wills took a lead off third base after the fourth steal, he saw Pirates catcher Smokey

Wills swipes his 102nd base of the year on October 3, 1962, in the club's third and final playoff game against the San Francisco Giants. He would notch two more steals later in the game, but the Dodgers still lost, 7-5, allowing the Giants to reach the World Series.

their flaws, Wills knew that if he could get on base, he could successfully steal bases. Dodgers coach Pete Reiser further helped instill that confidence in Wills.

"Reiser taught me that basestealing is a matter of confidence, even conceit," Wills said. "It's more than getting a good jump. It's being in the right

Burgess call for a pitch-out. Burgess then threw the ball toward Wills, who thought Burgess was trying to hit him in the head.

In a game against Houston, first baseman Norm Larker took repeated pickoff throws and slapped his glove hard against Wills' injured leg each time. He had a hematoma caused by internal bleeding from all of his excessive sliding. After Wills stole three bases against the Cubs, Cubs manager Charlie Metro threatened to walk the pitcher the next time he came up to clog up the bases.

As he had done a year earlier, when Maris was making a run at Babe Ruth's home run record, Commissioner Ford Frick ruled that for Wills to be considered the new stolen base champion, he would have to break Cobb's record in 154 games. It was discovered, however, that Cobb had actually played 156 games in 1915 because of two Detroit ties.

Wills reached 95 steals in his 154th game, then got the two he needed to pass Cobb in his 156th game of the season. The historic 100th steal came on September 27, against Houston.

When the Dodgers and Giants tied for the NL pennant, it set up a best-of-three game playoff series. It also gave Wills the opportunity to increase his total, since those games were considered part of the regular season.

After splitting the first two games, Wills did his best to try to carry the Dodgers to the pennant. He got four singles — half of the Dodgers' hits — off Juan Marichal on the day, following his 30th birthday. After his last hit, in the seventh, he stole second, and then third. When catcher Ed Bailey threw the ball into left field, Wills continued home

On September 7, Wills stole his 81st base to break the NL's single-season steals record previously held by Bob Bescher. The Dodgers presented Wills, who stole four bases in the game, with the bag as a memento.

to put the Dodgers in front, 4-2.

The applause for Wills was almost as loud as the cheers greeting the nearly simultaneous announcement of astronaut Wally Schirra's safe return from space. After orbiting the Earth six times in a Sigma 7 Mercury spacecraft, Schirra had splashed down in the Pacific Ocean, less than four miles from the recovery ship.

Before the fans could continue celebrating, however, the Giants pulled off a rally similar to 1951, scoring four runs in the ninth for a 6-4, pennant-winning victory.

Wills' final total of 104 steals was even more impressive in light of the fact that he was only thrown out 13 times. When Cobb set his mark in 1915, he had been thrown out 38 times.

Even more remarkable was the fact that Wills didn't just steal more bases than every other player in the majors — he stole more than every team as well. His closest challengers were the Washington Senators, who stole 99 bases, followed by the Cardinals, who collectively stole 86.

Wills did accomplish his goal of playing in every Dodger game, all 165 of them, but he failed to hit .300 — by one hit. His total of 208 hits in 695 at-bats left him with a .2992 average. If he had recorded just one more hit, he would have raised his average to .3007.